THE SOUL OF BLACK WALL STREET

PRESTIGE & ENTREPRENEURSHIP

LIBERTY & JUSTICE

International Bestselling Author

John A. Andrews

THE SOUL OF BLACK WALL STREET

Copyright © 2020 by John A. Andrews.
All rights reserved. Written permission must be secured from the publisher to use or reproduce any part of this book, except for brief quotations in critical reviews or articles.
Published in the U.S.A. by
Books That Will Enhance Your Life™
A L I - Andrews Leadership International
www.JohnAAndrews.com
Cover Design: John A. Andrews
Cover Graphic Designer: A L I
Cover Photo: Cerqueira & Youssef Naddam
Edited by: A L I
ISBN: 9798664303582

THE SOUL OF BLACK WALL STREET

Our deepest fear is not that we are inadequate.
Our deepest fear is that we are powerful beyond
measure.
It is our light, not our darkness that most frighten us.

We ask ourselves, who am I to be brilliant, gorgeous,
talented and fabulous?
Actually, who are you not to be?
You are a child of god. Your playing small doesn't
serve the world.

There's nothing enlightened about shrinking so that
other people won't feel insecure around you.
We were born to make manifest the glory of God that is
within us.
It's not just in some of us, it's in everyone.

And, as we let our own light shine, we unconsciously
give other people permission to do the same. As we are
liberated from our own fear, our presence automatically
liberates others.[1]

- Marianne Williamson

"I say to you today, my friends, though, even though we face the difficulties of today and tomorrow, I still have a dream. It is a dream deeply rooted in the American dream. I have a dream that one day this nation will rise up, live out the true meaning of its creed: "We hold these truths to be self-evident, that all men are created equal."

- Dr. Martin Luther King, Jr.

THE SOUL OF BLACK WALL STREET

TABLE OF CONTENTS

CHAPTER ONE..6
CHAPTER TWO..9
CHAPTER THREE..12
CHAPTER FOUR..16
CHAPTER FIVE..19
CHAPTER SIX..22
CHAPTER SEVEN..26
CHAPTER EIGHT...31
CHAPTER NINE...34
CHAPTER TEN...38
CHAPTER ELEVEN...41
CHAPTER TWELVE..46
CHAPTER THIRTEEN...50
CHAPTER FOURTEEN...54
CHAPTER FIFTEEN..60
CHAPTER SIXTEEN...64
CHAPTER SEVENTEEN...68
CHAPTER EIGHTEEN..72
CHAPTER NINETEEN..75
CHAPTER TWENTY...78
CHAPTER TWENTY-ONE..82
CHAPTER TWENTY-TWO...85
CHAPTER TWENTY-THREE..88
CHAPTER TWENTY-FOUR...92
CHAPTER TWENTY-FIVE..95
CHAPTER TWENTY-SIX..98
CHAPTER TWENTY-SEVEN...102

THE SOUL OF BLACK WALL STREET

PRESTIGE & ENTREPRENEURSHIP

1

As I embarked on writing this historical chronicle, I asked Invisible Guide for not only knowledge but also the wisdom to think as the pioneers of Black Wall Street did. As you read its pages, you will find a thread embedded within. I say: Grab it and weave your fabric, not for animus but success. If for some reason, you miss it on your first read. Try rereading the book until you find it and get busy. Let us explore the making of Black Wall Street.

IN 1921, TULSA, Oklahoma's Greenwood District known as Black Wall Street, beamed as one of the most prosperous African-American communities in the United States. How did it all begin? What was at its core?

In 1906, an astute character and wealthy Landowner who I dubbed **Willian T.** resigned his governmental position and left riotous Arkansas in the backdrop in search of socioeconomic progress.

Arkansas forever remained painted - a place where multiple black men were killed thus igniting the Argenta Race Riot.

He boards a bus carrying his attaché and carry-ons heading west toward Tulsa, Oklahoma. The driver, a white man, already seated in the driver's seat, notices as he boarded.

William T. sees a vacant front seat across from the driver. He lays one of his bags on it.

"Negro, there's a seat for you in the rear of the bus. You know you do not sit up front on any bus. Especially on my bus. Hurry, you may want to grab it so we can get going."

William T. heads to the rear of the bus with his luggage. Passengers on that mostly whites-bus eyed him with suspicion of - his desire to conquer. He occupies a window seat at the back of the bus next to a woman with a temper-tantrum toddler. Secures some luggage overhead and lands the attaché on the floor between his legs. The bus pulls away from the depot before he gets comfortable thereon. Hours later, after multiple stops, Tulsa entered into view.

2

Arriving in Tulsa and looking out that window, he notices a 40-acre lot. Subliminally, he saw the sign and internalized *to be sold only to coloreds*.
"On this slice of land, I will build a Black City. Not just a luxurious community but also one filled with pride, prestige, and entrepreneurship. In addition, it shall be called the – Black city of Commerce. We shall trade daily, not with the money of others but with ours. Even if it gets torched by the powers of white

supremacy – in the hearts, minds, and souls of Blacks, it shall remain in the psyche of our race."

The bus pulled up at a depot in the vicinity. Willian T. inadvertently debussed close to the train tracks and headed to the Motel across the street - displaying that black on white painted vacancy sign. He checked in, asking for a room with a view.

"Why do you need a view? The only thing here to see is the railroad tracks."

Said the White Attendant.

"Give that other negro what he asks. When it rains – it pours."

Said her Boss, sporting a tired Fu Manchu.

Landing in the room, William T. pulls back the window shades staring at the plot as the sun goes down and again in the morning as the sun comes up.

Previously, another African American entrepreneur, I call him *John The Baptist*, reminiscent of the one who preceded Christ, arrived in Tulsa, in 1899. He, deep down in his psyche, believed that black people had a better chance of economic progress if they pooled their resources together, worked together, and supported each other's businesses. He subsequently bought large tracts of real estate in the northeastern part of Tulsa, which he had subdivided and sold exclusively to other African Americans.

Born into slavery in Kentucky, John, an outspoken executive later there, became a lawyer and activist. He built a Hotel on Greenwood, where blacks could enjoy the amenities of the downtown hotels, which served only whites. It was said to be the largest black-owned hotel within the United States.

3

It was at the time when many blacks were migrating from Mississippi – thus avoiding harsh oppression.
During that late nineteenth-century social tensions surfaced and became defined in terms of rich versus poor, native-born versus immigrant in most of the U.S, and worker versus capitalist.

THE SOUL OF BLACK WALL STREET

Tensions continued to center on the relations between blacks and whites in those states tagged to the former Confederacy. Lynchings, black killings found its way – center stage despite all the calls for a New South, in the years after Reconstruction.

Although a small percentage of African-Americans found work in the new iron foundries and steel mills, they generally got barred from the textile mills that grew into the region's primary industry. Those mill owners preferred to use white women and children rather than blacks, who they increasingly portrayed as lazy, ignorant, and shiftless. Consequently, the overwhelming majority of African-Americans got bonded to the land as sharecroppers or tenant farmers.

By 1900, segregation became institutionalized throughout the South, and the civil rights of blacks were sharply curtailed after the Reconstruction.

Jim Crow laws and segregation became nefariously enacted. Under the Civil Rights Act of 1875, racial discrimination in public accommodations such as hotels, railroads, and theaters became prohibited to blacks. Segregated facilities, whether schools or public transportation, restaurants, hotels, etc., were rarely equal.

While several Southern states spent nearly the same amount on the education of whites and blacks in 1890, there was a tremendous disparity in spending in favor of whites within two decades. Legalized segregation also reinforced the notions of white racial superiority and African-American inferiority, creating an atmosphere that encouraged violence, and during the 1890s, those lynchings of blacks rose significantly. Despite these apparent problems, the Supreme Court did not overturn the concept of separate but equal until 1954.

The end of Reconstruction did not mean an end to African-American political influence in the South. However, Blacks continued to serve in several state legislatures as late as 1900. Some were even elected to Congress after 1877, although from all-black districts. However, a change took place in the 1890s as attitudes about race became severe. and the prospect of an electoral alliance between poor whites and blacks that could threaten the power structure became a possibility.

While the Fifteenth Amendment ensured that African-Americans could not be denied the right to vote, the southern states came up with various ways to disenfranchise blacks. A strategy still classified as Black Voter Suppression.

Relatedly, Mississippi's 1890 constitution imposed limitations on voting that were aimed primarily at African-Americans. These limitations included residency requirements, disqualification of individuals convicted of even minor crimes, payment of all taxes (including the poll tax), and a literacy test. Such loopholes existed within these restrictions to favor whites who might have been otherwise ineligible to vote. For example, an illiterate person who could demonstrate to the registrar that he "understood" the constitution would be allowed to vote.

Louisiana adopted the so-called **grandfather clause**, which allowed men to vote if their fathers or grandfathers had been eligible to vote as of January 1, 1867. No blacks had the right to vote anywhere in the South at that time. No, not one! Although the Supreme Court ultimately declared the grandfather clause unconstitutional, this and similar laws drastically cut African-American voter registration in the South by 1900.

Because of these and other depressionary tactics imposed upon them, most Blacks fled states such as Mississippi to Tulsa, Oklahoma. They were initiating the wave of the Great Migration of African-Americans, moving from the rural South to the urban North in the 1890s.

4

Willian T. arrival in Tulsa, along with that of other entrepreneurial black mindsets, coincided with this great migration. It was not about what you can do for me but instead what we can do collectively. It was all about reaching out and touching someone else. William T. owned the first black business in that black district of Greenwood in 1906 and taught others how to do likewise.

Conscious about the influx of blacks fleeing oppression from other states, he launched out with a boarding house located on a dusty trail near the railroad tracks. This road of prestige Greenwood Avenue and was named for a city in Mississippi. The area became very popular among African American migrants fleeing the oppression in Mississippi. They would find refuge in that building, as the racial persecution from the south was non-existent on Greenwood Avenue. There they found solace.

Committed to his vision of creating something for black people by black people – he loaned money to those who wanted to start a business.

It was not just his mindset, but another pioneer, John The Baptist, who built a 55 room luxury hotel and proudly etched his name on it. He later became the wealthiest African American in Tulsa via his rooming house, rental properties, and the largest African American-owned hotel in the United States.

John The Baptist initiated the development of Greenwood, referred to as the *Black Wall Street*.

I'll call this other black businessman/pioneer, A. J., who became part of their regular wealth-building meetings. He arrived there in the 1890s and later founded the local newspaper. This black-owned newspaper became instrumental in establishing that district's socially conscious mindset.

It was said:

"This newspaper regularly informed African Americans regarding their legal rights. Plus, any court rulings or legislation that were beneficial or harmful to the Greenwood District."

Back then, the demands for equal rights loomed while the oppression of Jim Crow laws still festered.

It was said of Greenwood:

"There was a railroad track running through it which separated the black and white populous."

Therefore, the reliance of a self-contained black economy came by design restraining each to their side of the tracks. Even though Black Wall Street was founded and developed by blacks, Tulsa was rigidly segregated, mainly after statehood in 1907.

5

These Black Wall Street executives not only met to determine how they could expand individual wealth but also discussed who needed money in their community. They realized that some were reluctant to ask for a loan. So, they sought them out and offered genuine support. William T. expressed resilience in making this happen. Providing not only lodging but also an opportunity for those escaping oppression in Mississippi was synonymous with his beliefs.

As time elapsed, it soon became a reality that the average income of black families was substantial. On that side of the tracks, a dollar circulated 36 to 100 times. It remained there in Greenwood for almost a year before leaving.

Meanwhile, Whites of that era equated improvement in wages and working conditions displayed in Black Wall Street as communistic threats. Coincidentally, they felt that slavery had flipped, blacks were now prime real estate owners, and they as whites were now second-class dwellers in their own homeland.

No doubt because of the white slave master mentality still existent within the white mindset, they saw themselves as the superior race. Even so, despite their inflated puffed-up perceptions of themselves, In Black Wall Street at this time resided several millionaires and many of substantial worth.

Several men and women were worth $100,000. While many had, possessions valued at $25,000 and $50,000. Yet, some are worth $25,000 and upward of $150,000. The meeting of such wealthy minds played an integral part in their amassing of such great fortunes.

Black businesses in this community benefited from such self-sufficiency. However, owing to the maintenance of the legality of racial societal challenges, in business, residential areas, education, and the entirety of segregation encouraged black initiative but also placed parameters on some African American opportunities.

Putting it another way, because it was unlawful for blacks to purchase from white-owned establishments, those black businesses boomed.

Even so, blacks were limited as to whatever business opportunities existent outside their district.

Yet, more impressively, six black families owned their own airplanes during that time, even though the state of Oklahoma only operated two airports.

Greenwood was home to far less-affluent African Americans as well. A significant number still worked in menial jobs, such as janitors, dishwashers, porters, and domestics. Yet, the money they earned outside of Greenwood was spent within the district.

6

From a series of their mastermind, wealth-building meetings not only emerged entrepreneurs but in the first two decades of the 20th century, Tulsa transformed from a dusty frontier into a thriving metropolis. Wealth gusher after gusher was discovered, and the city soon became the oil capital of the world.

THE SOUL OF BLACK WALL STREET

Between 1910 and 1920, Tulsa's population nearly quadrupled to more than 72,000, and the Black community rose from below 2,000 to almost 9,000.

By 1920, a perspiring walk through "Black Wall Street" meant traversing more than 35 bustling city blocks, with the locus being the intersection of Greenwood Avenue and Archer Street, adjacent to Tulsa's Frisco rail tracks.

The Acme Brick Company supplied building materials to the townhouses, apartments, theaters, and hotels that lined the streets. In addition, by 1910, Black bricklayers had their own trade union called the Hod Carriers Local 199.

Other entrepreneurs also began to emerge, such as John Williams and his wife, Loula. They soon built a confectionary store and erected the opulent Dreamland Theater.

Simon Berry built a private transportation network of Model T. Fords and buses, which transported residents through Greenwood and to downtown Tulsa. Berry soon began chartering planes for Tulsa's increasingly wealthy oilmen.

Though the population was relatively small, Greenwood also had two newspapers, including the Tulsa Star, founded by A.J. Others built pool halls, auto repair shops, beauty parlors, grocers, barbershops, and funeral homes. There was a Y.M.C.A and a roller-skating rink, a hospital, and a

U.S. post office substation. With all this activity, Greenwood's economy was gushing like one of Getty's wells.

Along with this massive prosperity, the community also invested in houses of worship and schools. By 1920, Greenwood had a handful of churches, most notably by the impressive Mt. Zion Baptist Church built in 1909 and founded by William T.

The district also had its own elite high school, named after Booker T. Washington, which boasted a curriculum that would prepare students to eventually study at colleges like Columbia in New York, Oberlin in Ohio, and historically Black colleges such as Hampton, Tuskegee, and Spelman.

Meanwhile, freshmen studied algebra, Latin, and ancient history, as well as core subjects like English, science, art, and music.

In the interim, sophomores took economics and geometry, while juniors advanced to chemistry and trade-oriented subjects such as civics and business spelling. Seniors studied physics and trigonometry, as well as vocal music, art, and bookkeeping.

So important was an education in upwardly mobile Greenwood that teachers were among the highest-paid workers. Many had their own Steinway pianos in their apartments, while the school's principal, E.W. Woods, lived in a six-room townhouse.

Amid this bustling landscape, William T. continued to expand his empire. At Greenwood's peak, he owned and rented out three brick apartment buildings and five townhouses near another one of his businesses, a grocery store. He then built the Hotel, started a Masonic lodge, and opened an employment agency for migrant workers. The Hotel, located at 112 N. Greenwood, the street's first commercial enterprise, valued at $55,000, with it Brunswick Billiard Parlor and Dock Eastmand & Hughes Cafe.

William T. also owned a two-story building at 119 N. Greenwood. It housed Carter's Barbershop, Hardy Rooms, a pool hall, and a cigar store. Additionally, he bought an 80-acre farm in Rogers County.

His property lines were Pine Street to the north, the Frisco rail tracks to the south, Lansing Avenue to the east, and Cincinnati Avenue to the west.

As Greenwood's premier entrepreneur, he built ties with residents in white Tulsa, just across the Frisco tracks, and eventually became sheriff's deputy, charged with policing the Black population.

7

Retrospectively, during slavery, Blacks labored for their masters - slave owners who were mostly white. Slaves were not permitted to own anything except for the clothes on their backs. Consequently, except for their minds, Blacks had no rights and no property back then. To put it subtly, their masters possessed them.

Foundationally, it has been over 400 years since Blacks were forced to the American continent against their will as slaves. Reportedly, in late August 1619, way before Jamestown, the *White Lion*, an English privateer commanded by John Jope, sailed into Point Comfort and dropped its anchor deep in the James River. According to the Virginia colonist John Rolfe who documented the arrival of the ship – there were at least twenty Africans on board.

The dramatic scene unfolded earlier when Captured in Africa; Slave traders forced these slaves to march for several hundred miles to the coast to board ships like the *San Juan Bautista* - one of at least 36 transatlantic Portuguese and Spanish slave ships.

Packed tightly on board with about 350 Africans like sardines in a tin, the ship sailed west. On each voyage, inevitably hunger and disease took a swift toll. Consequently, en route, about 150 slaves perished. With limited time and workforce at their avail, those corpses were thrown overboard to lighten the load and relinquish the stench.

On one occasion, when the *San Juan Bautista* approached the port of what is now Veracruz, Mexico in the summer of 1619, it faced off with two ships, the *White Lion* and another

English privateer, the *Treasurer*. The crews stormed the vulnerable slave ship and seized 50 to 60 of the remaining Africans. After, the pair sailed for Virginia in search of profits.

As documented by Rolfe, when the *White Lion* arrived in what is now present-day Hampton, Virginia, the Africans were off-loaded and bought for provisions, etc. The Governor, at that time, Sir. George Yeardley and head merchant Abraham Piersey acquired the majority of the slaves, most of whom got detained in **Jamestown,** which became America's first permanent settlement.

When Blacks arrived in Tulsa, Oklahoma, after fleeing oppression, few of them were loaded financially. While some took on the expedition as a visionary quest, they collectively used the power of the mastermind. It was not the mind of their masters who kept them enslaved even after the emancipation of slavery – it was their own which, they possessed even before their capture in Africa.

Something amazingly powerful occurs when one realizes the potential they have in their toolbox and uses it. Most blacks get blessed with the iceberg syndrome – a good one. Ten percent of their potential is what you see, and all they see as well.

However, underneath the water, they are not only loaded but also as solid as a rock prospectively. That's one of the reasons why those slave masters still wanted to possess us (blacks) even after the abolishment of slavery.

Even so, we fail to grab our portion of this world's wealth because we allow jealousy and petty stuff to keep us away from the pot of gold. Some of us feel that we do not deserve a slice even if that cake is so massive and could accommodate everyone's fork – whether metal or plastic.

When the character William T. landed in Tulsa, Oklahoma, in 1906, he knew that he deserved that 40-acre plot. At the time, he did not know precisely how Black Wall Street was going to get built.

However, as he traded minds with other like-minded individuals – what they constructed became epic.

It is said:

"A mind is a terrible thing to waste."

I'll say, and you can quote me:

Our mind is our most powerful asset. Like a ship's rudder, we can manipulate it and steer it to whatever destination we desire. Of course, we must train it to withstand the rough seas, the tidal waves, the treacherous icebergs, the reefed shores, the other ships' white-water, the pitch-black lighthouse, and those on-coming ships aimed at a head-on collision and even targeted missiles.

Some people like to watch things happen, some people like to wonder what will happen, and some people do not care what happens. However, the action-driven person delights in making things happen.

When William T. left Arkansas, he was determined to make things happen. It was not a mere wish but a quest for William T., who resigned from his governmental position and became a BWS character. That white bus driver did not deter him.

John the Baptist left his law office in Mississippi amid white oppression. While A. J. moved to the Indian Territory from Alabama with his parents in the 1890s. A press pioneer, who distributed the first Democratic, African-American newspaper in Oklahoma, became a prominent voice on BWS.

A. C., another BWS character, dubbed as a clean-cut character, and one of the most notable surgeons in America, developed a net worth of over $100,000. Worth over $500,000, J.W. Thompson and others joined that league of Black Wall Street executives. As someone said, they burnt their bridges. They set sail even if the lighthouse grew dark. Every pioneer has this aptitude, and at times, it seems as if it got embedded inside their D.N.A.

Too many of us drift away with the wrong crowd going nowhere, fast. Those pioneers of Black Wall Street became a brand for doing things.

When they saw something that ought to be accomplished, they stepped up to the plate and hit the home run. To them, it was all, or it is nothing. They had burnt their ships.

Those pioneers acquired the action habit, and others had no choice but to step aside for them to advance.

They took one step forward in the direction of their goals and dreams, and adversaries ran for cover.

When these men walked into a board meeting and departed after shaking hands, whatever they discussed was considered – accomplished.

9

We live in a world full of half-alive people who no longer believe in themselves. Alive at age 35 but mentally, most are already dead and buried. The extraordinary life eludes them. Any professional bodybuilder would tell you that a muscle only grows when it is stretched. The sleeping giants within those BWS pioneers became alive.

It is said:

THE SOUL OF BLACK WALL STREET

Those who have no central purpose in life fall easy prey to petty worries, fears, troubles, and self-pitying, all of which are indications of weakness, which lead just as surely as deliberately planned sins (though by a different route) to failure, unhappiness, and loss. For weakness cannot persist in a power-evolving universe. We should conceive of a legitimate purpose in our hearts and set out to accomplish it.

Theirs was an economic war to be fought. Yes, lifting their heads above the crowd gave them purpose, ammunition, and direction in life. They saw where they needed to go. In addition, the world always seems to make way for the person who knows where he or she is going. Streets are crowded; a fire engine is coming. Everything gives way. They all step aside for this speeding machine on a mission. Why? It has a purpose – putting out the fire, and it has a sense of urgency in doing so.

THE CHAMPION

The average runner sprints
Until the breath in him is gone
But the champion has the iron will
That makes him "carry on.

For rest, the average runner begs
When limp his muscles grow
But the champion runs on leaden legs

His spirit makes him go.

The average man's complacent
When he does his best to score
But the champion does his best
And then he does a little more.

- Author unknown.

A purpose-driven individual will readily discover within that "extra-ness" necessary to overcome all odds. The words "I can't" are eliminated from his or her vocabulary. Whenever confronted with any sign of defeat, he resolves:
"I am not giving up, bring it on. It might lick some, but not me. I absolutely will not be denied!"
Author Julia Cameron writing in her book **The Artist's Way** says,
"I have learned, as a rule of thumb, never to ask whether you can do something. Say, instead, that you are doing it. Then fasten your seat belt. The most remarkable thing follows. " Additionally, she states, *"Take a small step in the direction of a dream and watch the synchronous doors flying open."* **A maxim worth remembering**, *"Leap, and the net will appear."*
That door opened for William T. He visualized, making that 40-acre plot into a city for blacks. With the help of other black business people, he was able to

do just that. One day while he was walking through that Greenwood District, he saw the need for a hospital. The rest became history.

10

William T. saw what he wanted and embarked upon accomplishing it. Thus amazing things occurred. If we were to interview purpose-driven individuals, they no doubt will take away the excuses of many, including ours. It is a given: Most people lack the initiative necessary to fulfill their destiny. They have flunked; mainly because they do not believe deep down inside that, they are valuable. Therefore, they live a purpose-deprived life instead of a purpose-driven one.

Purpose, a *directive* word, which means heading towards something, gains momentum when meshed with the *propellant* word belief – that feeling of knowing that you can do whatever you set out to do. People, lacking the fuel in their mindset and philosophy, usually look for this additive coming from someone else's, and when they don't receive it, they wonder why their life spins around like a top in mud – going nowhere fast. To take advantage of others believing in you, you must first harness the power of belief in yourself.

When a commercial airplane is getting ready for takeoff, first, the doors are closed shut. Then the push back. With Passenger's, seat belts securely fastened. The plane then taxis down the runway in preparation for takeoff. The air traffic controllers in the control tower are aware the flight is ready for takeoff. Instruction given to the pilot to speed up. The pilot releases the throttle, retracts the landing gear, and engages the skies.

Believing in yourself will initiate purpose. **Belief – that ability necessary to taxi down the runway in preparation for takeoff**.

As soon as William T. began believing in themself, others started believing in him – his ascent became eminent. *All things are possible to those who believe*. The

BWS executives were driven by that burning desire to succeed. They knew where they were going and consequently found their hidden guides to take them there. It is a truism,

"When the student is ready, the teacher appears."

11

The truism screams: **Timing** is everything. When William T. landed in Tulsa, Oklahoma, and noticed that 40-acre plot for sale, the history of a Black Wall Street began taking shape.

The famous axiom states: The "T" in *timing* is better than the "T" in *talent*. If the sun misses its appointment with planet earth, we could, for a long time be in utter darkness. If the waves miss their timing, the ocean will swallow us up with a tsunami.

Timing has a lot to do with synchronicity but more so with preparedness. William T. was not only adept at preparation, but he also relied on his intuition to capitalize on his ideas. Philosopher, Benjamin Disraeli says,

"The secret of success in life is for a man to be ready for his time when it comes."

Abraham Lincoln, on one of the biggest failures in his life, said:

"Give me six hours to chop down a tree, and I will spend the first four sharpening the ax."

Bottom line, because William T. was prepared, and the right opportunity presented itself, he seized it and dominated. That is what others call luck. That is success at the utmost – the way a high achiever performs.

Most high achievers love what they do and are at their best doing so. They allow their creativity to operate at the max. Conversely, so many people allow their creativity to be caged up doing things they detest doing - only because it pays the bills. While William T boarded that bus, many remained in Arkansas, nurturing a wish instead of the dream.

Most successful people are not lucky; they just master the law of timing. It means they are always taking action in some way or another.

THE SOUL OF BLACK WALL STREET

As William T. and others on BWS strived to realize their vision, many wannabes criticized and or called them lucky.

Philosopher, James Allen says:

"The thoughtless, the ignorant, and the indolent seeing the apparent effects of things and not the things themselves, talk of luck, of fortune, and of chance. Seeing others grow rich, they say, 'How lucky they are!' Observing others become intellectual, they exclaim, 'How highly favored they are!' Moreover, noting the saintly character and wide influence of still others, they remark, 'How chance aids them at every turn!' They do not see the trials, failures, and struggles, which these people have voluntarily encountered to gain their experience; not know the sacrifices they have made, of the undaunted efforts they have put forth, of the faith they have exercised, that they might overcome the insurmountable and realize the vision of their heart. They do not know the darkness and the heartaches; they only see the light and joy and call it "luck," They do not see the long and arduous journey but only behold the pleasant goal and call it "good fortune." They do not understand the process but only perceive the result and call it "chance."

Those BWS pioneers realized a vision provides the fuel or the belief to see it come true. Keeping that vision alive, though, is imperative because there is always going to be the naysayer(s) who will tell you that you do not have what it takes to make it a reality. You may excitedly launch your ship and understand that those winds and storms are going to come billowing against you. Trusting their possible caring attitude, you can make that mistake of lending a deaf ear to your unused capacity crying out within you, saying, **"You can do it!"** So many missed opportunities occur from failure to listen to that still small voice. That voice, like a great friend prodding an individual on through the tough times. Those times when others lose belief in *them*.

Do you know someone who started something but failed to finish? Someone who got straight "A's" now all they get are "F's"? Those pioneers did not fall into that trap because it is always fully baited with excuses, waiting for failures bent on quitting. They launched their dream of Black Wall Street solely bent on helping other coloreds and pursued it with reckless abandon.

Harriet Beecher Stowe declares:

"When you get into a tight place and everything goes against you, 'til it seems as though you could not hold on a minute longer. Never give up then, for that is just the place and time that the tide will turn."

You are and will continually become acquainted with blacks who, because of their uniqueness, acquired their unique brand of success. Driven by an extraordinary determination to achieve their goals at all costs – they excelled despite systematic injustice.

Every opposition brought them closer to a "YES." They became adept at turning setbacks of slavery-related incidents into comebacks of equality. The people were so loyal to each other when it came down to maintaining the prosperous attitude in Greenwood that they traded with each other instead of doing so elsewhere. If customers requested an item that was NLA, that merchant would place an order for such, and they would wait until it arrived.

It is said:

"Nothing in the world can take the place of persistence. Talent will not. Nothing is more common than unsuccessful men with talent. Genius will not. Unrewarded genius is almost a proverb. Education will not. The world is full of educated derelicts.

Persistence, determination, and hard work make a difference."

— Calvin Coolidge

12

William T. and those other pioneers at Black Wall Street were granted the opportunities to get out of their ocean to see what differentiates them. Based on the world's population of almost seven billion people, who stands out? Those blacks did not reason – Really. Me? No Way! That is impossible. I am nobody. I do not have the brains. I am from the wrong side of the tracks. I was born into slavery. I do not have what it takes. I am not the best tool in the shed. I am not, I am not, and I am not.

William T. and others saw it differently. Instead, they negated holding onto those false beliefs about themselves – Understanding, those are nothing but figments of your imagination.

Whenever they are looking at a collection of pictures, they looked for and see themselves within. They saw themselves as unique in this day and time. They saw and felt the power of advancement. They had already tested the mettle and found that they had unlimited potential to become successful.

What if you were told that have within the power to become successful? That you have at this moment, an ability that lays dormant, like an inactive volcano, and when discovered and tapped into, it will erupt and lift you from failure to success in a blaze of glory.

This power can assist in transforming anyone into a person who can experience tremendous influence and success. This might be hard to believe, comprehend, or figure out. They have shown you that all you have to do is to trust **your** power by *knowing yourself?*

In his book ***On Becoming a Leader,*** Warren Bennis writes,

"Know thyself, then, means separating who you are and who you want to be from what the world thinks you are and wants you to be."

It is a given that KNOWLEDGE IS POWER. However, Self-knowledge is your first key to success. When true self-knowledge emerges, one understands that the sky is the limit to potential! Knowing that they have the power alone will keep them up at night.

They become captivated by such a burning desire to tap into and unleash that 90% unused potential. William T. and the other entrepreneurs at Black Wall Street, no doubt, were continually planning the next series of moves for their life.

Unfortunately, and tragically, as human beings, we place very little value on ourselves and subsequently acclimatize toward failure. We live in a world bombarded with negative news, pessimism, and a mediocrity mindset. As a result, devaluing ourselves has become such an easy thing to do. Watching the constant negative report for a few hours over some time, and we are hooked, immersed in all that negativity. As the saying goes,

"Garbage in garbage out. So the hard drive in our computer – our mind is programmed."

We fear our own potential resulting in living our life hiding our light from not only ourselves but the world.

To, once again quote - Marianne Williamson:

Our deepest fear is not that we are inadequate.
Our deepest fear is that we are powerful beyond measure.
It is our light, not our darkness that most frighten us.

THE SOUL OF BLACK WALL STREET

We ask ourselves, who am I to be brilliant, gorgeous, talented and fabulous?
Actually, who are you not to be?
You are a child of god. Your playing small doesn't serve the world.

There's nothing enlightened about shrinking so that other people won't feel insecure around you.
We were born to make manifest the glory of God that is within us.
It's not just in some of us, it's in everyone.

And, as we let our own light shine, we unconsciously give other people permission to do the same. As we are liberated from our own fear, our presence automatically liberates others.

13

By the turn of 1913, more business people gravitated to Black Wall Street, including lawyers and doctors. The offices of Buck Colbert Franklin and A.C. Jackson stood tall, Plus, Dunbar and Booker T. Washington schools, Vernon A.M.E., and Mount Zion Baptist churches, Ricketts' Restaurant, The Williams' Dreamland Theater, Mann's Grocery Stores, Stratford Hotel, and a host of haberdasheries, drug stores, cafes, barbershops and beauty salons. Business attracting massive black patronage.

In the interim, the infamous educator Booker Taliaferro Washington aka Booker T. visited Tulsa for the dedication of a small school named in his honor. He became ecstatic visiting the business district of Greenwood; stoked by the entrepreneurial spirit of the Greenwood residents he became acclimated. Many claimed: Booker T. Washington earned the credited for coining the phrase - the Negro Wall Street of America. Later tagged the Black Wall Street – this affluent black community became one to be reckoned with. Just as success attracts friends, it also attracts enemies. Subliminally, the seeds of hatred marinated.

DURING 1918, the Greenwood District evolved as a booming community. Proud of its population with an individual school system. While most kids learned Black History along with other subjects, entrepreneurship engulfed them as a way of life.

One day, while William T. was leaving the bank, he saw a group of school kids across the street feasting on ice cream.

"Howdy, Mr. T."

They said in chorus.

He acknowledged them with a wave of the hand.

Junior, a pre-teen and ardent fan of his, rendered a styled military salute.
"Hey, Junior! How's school?"
William T. asked.
"School is great. Learning about where I came from."
Junior says.
"That's great. And where was that?"
Asks William T.
"From **Sierra Leone,** our ancestors came in on a ship. They were beaten, chained, and loaded onto the ship with tiny quarters…"
"Tell him they got packed like sardines in a can."
Says one of his peers.
"He got the picture."
Junior responds.
"And how are you going to change all that, Junior?"
William T. asks.
"We are going to get paid!"
Junior says, with his peers prompting him on with high-fives.
"That's right."
William T. responds.
"Yep. Do not forget to collect it from the white man. They owe us. They have defaulted on their promissory note. Tell them they need to pay up along with interest. Forty acres and a mule!"
Junior says.
His peers are stunned regarding Juniors' bravado.

THE SOUL OF BLACK WALL STREET

"I will!"
William T. says as he gets into his chic automobile.
Tommy Tillis, from across the tracks, views the scene
from his bedroom window through a viewfinder.

14

The music plays soulfully by the band and reverberates. Partiers revel in their chic attire. On the outside top-of-the line-automobiles roll up, and patrons exit entering the lavish restaurant. Valet parkers accommodate. The all-black band steps up its game, dropping some of the latest hits. The bandleader announces the upcoming intermission and makes a toast to the entrepreneurs of Black Wall Street and the opening of the new Williams' Theatre.

The bandleader reminds them to hold onto their champagne glasses for the ribbon-cutting ceremony. During the intermission, the crowd moves next door to the newly built Williams Dreamland Theatre. William T. cheers the event along with John Williams, A. J., and John the Baptist. The huge scissors held by Julia Williams severs the red fabric.

After the ribbon-cutting event, the band returns to the small restaurant stage and continues its stellar performance. John Williams tarries outside the theatre for photo Ops. Mrs. Williams rejoins the crowd on the inside.

The valet parking attendant comes up to John Williams. They are now engaged in a lengthy conversation. Meanwhile, Tom Tillis, from across the tracks along with his wife Betsy Tillis, remains busily occupied – covertly counting all those chic automobiles. They are attired as if attending the party. Even though not invited to this all-colored event.

"Send him over."

Says John Williams.

The valet attendant walks over to Tom Tillis and his wife and escorts them in the direction of John Williams. In the interim, John Williams' bodyguards presses and take up their position nearby.

"What can I do for you?"
Asks John Williams.
"Howdy. I am Betsey Tillis. This is my husband, Tom Tillis. We live across the railroad tracks…"
"I have seen you a couple of times, Tom."
Says John Williams, interrupting.
"Congrats on the opening of your new theatre. We came by to find out if you would be interested in selling it. If not now, but at some point? Or even operating it on a partnership basis?"
Betsy Tillis says.
"That could be a great deal for all of us. I call it a win, win. Plus, we don't yet have a theatre across those railroad tracks. Would that be something you would be up to?"
Says Tom Tillis.
"I don't think that is going to be a good deal, Tom Tillis. However, I commend you for your defiance. Here in the Greenwood District, it's for coloreds only. The laws of segregation are still in place, remember?"
Says John Williams.
"Johnny?"
"No. Call me Williams or John Williams."
Says John Williams
Tom Tillis tips his cigar and empties the ash into the ashtray outside the theatre. In the interim, a few patrons exit the restaurant, and the music from inside crescendo.

"We don't have to abide by all of that. Those laws of yesterday could get swept under the rug. Moreover, if we were to work this out together, we could make Tulsa into a much stronger community. Right now, with a second theatre, you are poised to make a profit. Even so, with our involvement, we could double the benefits and shift some traffic to the other building. Instead of limited daily operation, we could turn it into a twenty-four-hour operation. Thereby, profits will skyrocket. Don't you see?"
Says Tom Tillis.
"Tom. I hear - you. However, you need to talk with A. J. He owns the newspapers. Nothing happens in Greenwood unless he has a say in it."
Says John Williams.
"You boys are living it up. Tom, what did we miss along the way? How do you all maintain six airplanes?"
Asks Betsy Tillis.
Coincidentally, A. J., and William T. walk outside without even being summoned.
"Tom Tillis, this is A. J., the man you need to talk with concerning the theatre."
Says John Williams.
A. J. introduces himself. So does William T.
Tom Tillis restates his mission without hesitation, expecting the big win, aided by the prodding of his wife Betsy, now swinging her pocketbook.

"Tom Tillis. No need to beat around the bush. I am a straight shooter. If you do not believe me, you can read it in the News tomorrow in both of our papers. We are not about to build up this town with another race. Those theatres are for coloreds only, as John Williams told you. Those are our rules."
Says A. J.
"And John Tillis, let me restate: Those are the rules."
The bodyguard ensemble reinforced and flanks the Black executives.
"We heard from you. However, if you change your mind, please let us know. We will give you a pretty penny for it. Have a good night."
Says Tom Tillis. He begins departing along with his wife, Betsy.
"We say what we mean and mean what we say. You can read it in the News."
Says A. J.
Tom Tillis is not a happy camper. One could discern the body language of a let down on his face. Betsy is now several footsteps ahead of him as he lags.
"Come on, Tom! Do not worry. Those niggas are going to change their minds. How dear they talk down to us like that. If it were not for us, those boys would have nothing. We brought them out of Africa. We gave them liberty off the plantations."
Says Betsy.

"You are right. They are going to regret it. Give me some time. We will have all those Negroes underneath our thumb soon. I blame Abraham Lincoln for giving them what they don't deserve."

The couple now arrives on their side of the tracks.

15

On that following morning, several students crowded inside the assembly hall. After the principal's pep talk, the featured speaker from among the student body got introduced – Junior Rowland. As he graced the stage, applause erupted. Junior quiets the audience. He approached the podium ideally suited for his height.

My name is Junior Rowland, but you can call me Junior. I guess because I am still 13 years old. When I turn 18, I hope to change it if my mother can let go of it. "Junior! Junior! You have messed up again. When are you going to comport? Before I could say Mah...? Watch your words, Junior. This is still the white man's country. Slavery got abolished, but the rules are still in effect."

I hear her, but I do not see the justification in this completely Jim Crow law, still chasing the black race. Jim Crow, like a rooster, crowed excessively loud. He woke up the progressive black people and sent them straight to Tula, Oklahoma, where they created Greenwood – the Black Wall Street. I am here to let you know this morning that we are not here because of the oil surge but because of that rooster.

We may not be residing in the financial district in New York, but we value the Greenwood District. I do. No wonder we call it Greenwood. Green, the color of money – colored people money. I have a hunch! They are going to try to take it away from us. They owe us. Yet, they want more. As I stand here today, our list of enemies keeps growing. If they cannot organize from across the tracks, they are willing to recruit.

Junior gets much support from his peeps, who is always part of his entourage – and continues.

Do not be surprised; they are tooting to escalate that dirty word – lynching. You know it is coming to Greenwood when right here in Tulsa, the whites are not only lynching blacks; they are lynching their own race.

Last week in Washington, DC, rioting broke out and lasted for more than one week – July 19 – 24. It began in the wake of a rumor that a black man had raped a white woman. White men, many of whom were in the armed forces, took up their A.M.U. and launched into mob attacks on black individuals and businesses.

Ironically, The Washington D.C. Police Department refused to intervene, insisting blacks handle the situation and protect themselves. The police, for once, knew something smelled funky. After four days of police inaction, President Woodrow Wilson, who could not tame the Spanish Flu, called in 2,000 federal troops to pour cold water on the drama in the city. In the aftermath of this riot, 150 people were injured, and 15 killed.

If we were to travel back in time and lynch every slave master who raped our black sisters – we would be in the lynching business for decades.

I am almost two years from my fifteenth birthday, but I have seen enough. I have also read enough about the suppression tactics of the white man. They have suppressed the vote. They have suppressed our wealth until Greenwood. Yes, for years, they have been suppressing our potential.

They do not realize that we are as stable as an iceberg. They only see a fraction of us – but watch out. Watch out. I say watch out! They push us down, and we will rise again. Someday, if not in our lifetime our kid's lifetime or their kid's lifetime, we will put a black man in the white house.

THE SOUL OF BLACK WALL STREET

One who will show the Woodrow Wilson's of America how to lead? We will produce, leader after leader until they just let us be. I say, let us be!
The audience of school kids – echo.
He reverberates – *Just let us be! Thank God, we have defeated the pangs of slavery. We will overcome! I say we will overcome.*
Initiated by Junior's peers seated on the front row, the assembly room reverberates with a standing ovation.

17

Success boomed in 1920 and sustained it in 1921. William T. and his BWS associates continued enhancing that Greenwood District – they were also attracting some white enemies. Early that year they opened the Mount Zion Baptist Church. Meanwhile, nefariously, across the railroad tracks, those whites were plotting against them.

THE SOUL OF BLACK WALL STREET

When the blacks went to church on Sundays and thanked God for his blessings, folks across the railroad tracks held barbecues and other related gatherings – focusing on throwing a wrench into BWS. Meanwhile, back on August 4, 1916, Tulsa passed an ordinance that mandated residential segregation by forbidding blacks or whites from residing on any block where three-fourths or more of the residents were of the other race. However, Tom Tillis felt he was above the law.

Accordingly, although the United States Supreme Court declared such an ordinance unconstitutional, the following Tulsa, as well as many additional border and Southern cities, continued to establish and enforce segregation for the forthcoming three decades.

While all these ordinances marinated in the Greenwood Districts, the entertainment across the railroad tracks continued mainly to discuss the strides made by blacks on the other side of the tracks. At their B.B.Q. sessions, a frequent visitor was the 17-year-old Sarah Page, an elevator operator. Photographs of black lynchings always circulated. Sarah frequented most of those events. Some claimed Page was a divorcee.

Meanwhile, the affluence of African Americans in that Greenwood District became a topic of discussion. It attracted the attention of local white residents. They, at this point, were marinating resentment regarding the upscale lifestyle of people they deemed to be an inferior race—the word jealousy considered as appropriate during this time.

If you have particularly poor whites, who are looking at this prosperous community, which has large homes, beautiful furniture, crystals, china, linens, etc., the reaction is 'they don't deserve that.

As that jealousy fermented, Black Wall Street soon became an attraction with the resurgence of the Ku Klux Klan. Coincidentally, Blacks in Greenwood feared racial violence and the removal of their voting rights.

The Oklahoma Supreme Court for years routinely upheld the state's restrictions on voting access for African Americans, subjecting them to the poll tax and literacy tests. Meanwhile, lynching increased across the country, particularly during the Red Summer of 1919, where anti-black riots erupted in major cities across the United States, including Washington D.C, Chicago, and Tulsa.

So, in response, to the black lynching, an article in the black-owned newspaper *The Tulsa Star*, encouraged blacks to take up arms and to show up at courthouses and jails to make sure blacks who were on trial were not taken and killed by white lynch mobs.

The Tula Star, the newspaper founded by A. J., also regularly informed African Americans about their legal rights in court rulings. Moreover, or legislation that was beneficial or harmful to their community. Demands for equal rights evolved and simmered as an ongoing mission for blacks in Tulsa despite Jim Crow oppression.

17

In 1921, White supremacists took part in the murder of over 300 Blacks, torched their properties, including 600 businesses, 21 churches, 21 restaurants, 30 grocery stores, 2 movie theaters, 1 hospital, 1 bank. Moreover, its school system facilitates multiple schools, including The Booker T. Washington High School. On Memorial Day that weekend, the Greenwood District, known as Black Wall Street, came to a screeching halt. All of a sudden, that 40-acre community built up by an eclectic group of black pioneers saw its gears frozen in time, except for thousands of blacks running for their lives.

Days before, on the morning of May 21, 1921, a black shoeshine boy Dick Rowland wanted to use the restroom. In the building where he worked because of segregation, blacks were prohibited from using the restrooms used by whites.

Rowland needed to use a lavatory. He entered the Drexler Building across the street at 319 S. Main Street – which housed a blacks-only restroom on the top floor. It remains oblivious what happened on the elevator, except Sarah Page, that elevator operator was on duty. Seemingly, the elevator bucked, causing Sarah Page to lurch forward as a result in Rowland's direction. In that heat of the moment, Sarah shouted out in surprise.

Coincidentally, that moment transformed into Dick Rowland's death sentence. He sped out of the Drexler's building as fast as he could, anticipating no one saw him. Coincidentally, somebody heard the white girl's scream and saw this black boy running away from the building. Like the toss of a coin, it landed on heads – Dick Rowland's.

Dick Rowland had a few years ago dropped out of the Booker T. Washington High School.

Moments later, Rowland got arrested and incarcerated in Tulsa's County Courthouse. Suddenly, the scene of – *who let the dogs out* evolved and demanded justice. First on their minds – the lynching of Rowland.

Sarah Page, on the other hand, bore no identifying marks of even a struggle. Her clothing did not also appear torn or dislodged. No semen was found on or near her undergarments. No masculine scent mixed with hers - evaporated. Moreover, in her statement, Sarah refused to sign that she was raped or an altercation occurred.

Even so, the police insisted such was the case. Whites, already, simmering with marinated jealousy, refused to wait for the investigative process to unfold. As mentioned previously in this chronicle, for years, White Tulsan's had seen the rise of Black Wall Street and finally found a rope they could tie to that Greenwood district and pull it down in the depths of Hell.

Firstly, with the lynching of Dick Rowland. As they demanded, a noose is tied around his neck. At that time, over 3000 people in Tulsa were part of the K.K.K. The Tulsa Tribune, a white supremacist newspaper, ignited and dominated the press, headlined: *A Negro Assaults a White Girl*. Followed up by the talking point: *To Lynch a Negro Tonight*. The newspaper even referred to Rowland as "Diamond Dick."

THE SOUL OF BLACK WALL STREET

In the interim, an angry white mob surrounded the courthouse demanding that the sheriff hand over Dick Rowland – the sheriff refused.

Meanwhile, several men from across the railroad tracks in the Greenwood district resented what got spun in that white media. They had heard of far too many black lynchings, and this one was not going to contribute to the higher and deeper scenario.

In response, the Tulsa Star, the black-owned newspaper, had always encouraged blacks to take up arms and show up at the courthouses and jails to ensure blacks who were on trial were not taken and killed by those awful lynch mobs.

18

Later, that day a large mob formed around the jail in Tulsa, where Dick Rowland was jailed. As rumors of a potential lynching circulated throughout the Greenwood District, a group of about 75-armed men marched to the jail to protect him.
There they encountered at least 1500 whites.
"Where are you going with that gun nigga?"
Asked, a leader of the white mob.

"Don't worry. I will use it if I have to."
The black gun holder responded.
"Oh, No. You aren't."
Says the White man.
Tensions flared between blacks and whites and local power brokers, including William T., tried but failed to make peace. There was a scuffle between a white man and a Black man, resulting in a shot fired, and a little after 10 p.m. a riot had broken out.
Additional White Tulsans who did not have guns stole guns and ammunition from gun shops and headed for Greenwood. More than 1000 structures, including homes, got destroyed as planes flew overhead apparently fire-bombing Black Wall street. Homes were destroyed. Homes looted. Whites also took anything worth the taking.
A young white girl later appeared with a pack of chewing gum. When her parents asked her where she got it from, she said:
"Over at the N… Town."
As blacks returned to the area, they were not only restricted from gaining access but realized that what remained of their valued possession was now in the homes of many whites in Tulsa.
The human toll included over 300 blacks, buried and tortured because of the color of their skin. Plus, thousands of displaced residents.

Additionally, many of those residents passed through Tulsa's busy streets, and they held hands. Knowing they would not return to the houses, they had on the previous day, but to ashes.

19

John the Baptist was not present on the scene preceding the riot. As a tremendously successful executive, John shared the sentiment that he would never bow down or be subservient to anyone of the white race. John had previously refused to accept Booker T. Washington's buy-in approach that John worked on the conversion of Blacks as the best way to get along with whites. Subliminally, it seemed Booker T. felt that blacks should embark on kissing up to create a level playing field when it came down to race relations. As the pre-teen Junior, voiced previously to William T. one of John's associates:

"Whites had not fulfilled their promissory note. Forty acres and a mule?"

So, this strategy in John the Baptist's purview became dead on arrival.

Junior was heading from school, and witnessed the entire onslaught, as a white man riding in an ice wagon. The white man used the N-word along with some other derogatory comments. Juniors' wish came true when John the Baptist dislodged the man from the cart and pounded him until he fell to the ground. He embarked on beating the living daylights out of him.

John the Baptist unwinding looked across at the young boy.

"Hey, son, what is your name?"

"They call me Junior Rowland. I am thirteen years old, going on fourteen. I want to represent the Tulsa community. Become the voice of this black Greenwood District someday."

"I hear you, kid. Let me know how I can help."

John the Baptist returns to the beating of the white man. Junior seemed to have poured some gasoline on his onslaught. In the interim, John Williams ran out of the newly built Williams Dreamland Theater and pulled John the Baptist off the now hobbling white victim. Junior and his classmates became established cheerleaders. The white man whisked away pledging there would be a lynching that night in Tulsa. That threat was by now their common talking point. Fearing some backlash, Williams volunteered to drive John the Baptist away from the area. John remained resilient, not dreading any pushback.

By the early morning of June 1, 1921, an armed white mob had already started burning Greenwood to the ground.

During the torching, John the Baptist became a human shield for his infamous Stratford Hotel standing out front with his gun, waiting for the white mob to emerge. Despite his bravado, his hotel eventually went up in flames.

20

A black mother of a lighter shade reported the following episode: While in the house reading, her little girl was jumping up excitedly like a kid in a candy store.
"Mother, look at the cars full of people!"
"Don't disturb me when I am reading. I thought I told you that."

She said as she cozied up more comfortably with the book.
Then the little girl said:
"Mother, I see men with guns."
That got her attention.
She then went to the window and looked out. She saw numerous white men gathering in the Square.
It was then that the mother grabbed her little girl and rushed downstairs. They saw white men talking excitedly. Over 500 black men marched up to the jail. Moments later, a gunshot went off. Then a black man was shot right there on Main Street. This incident seemed to have gotten everyone's attention.
Moments later, three ambulances pulled up. The white mob turned on them.
"Don't touch the N...."
Yelled one white man.
The ambulance drivers were bewildered. So, they turned off their engines and remained double-parked in withdrawal.
The Police department commissioned over 500 deputies – the criteria they had to be white. A fair-skinned black man got summoned and then at least 50 others of his kind follow suit.
The command cchocd:
"Now you can go out and shoot any black man, and the law would be behind you."

Moments later, a whistle sounded, and airplanes flooded the skies dropping turpentine bombs. It was similar to when the Germans invaded Belgium, the mother recounted.

Meanwhile, on the ground, over 5000 white men fired their guns from all directions after that second whistle.

Black men, women, and children hastened to flee in safety. It was pandemonium as they got met on all sides with multiple rounds of ammunition. Men with torches ignited building after building. My daughter and I remained out of harm's way hidden behind the large pillar across from the police station.

"Where are those fire engines, when we need them – Mother?"

My little girl asked.

"With all these people here, I am sure they are stuck in traffic."

She responded.

However, we could hear the sirens echoing in the distance.

We saw trucks pull up, some of them even jumping the curb on Main Street. White men rushed out, and they began loading pianos and other expensive furniture onto them — everything of value they hauled from these homes.

We dared not go back to our home. Blacks were coming out of homes and buildings, but none were going in.

Additionally, all the cash found on them - they took. They even removed rings from their fingers, watches from their wrists, and snatched their chains from around their necks.

As the Greenwood District burned, the looting continued. During the riot, the white mob systematically looted each home before torching it. They cut the telephone lines and even blockade the railroad. There was no way to communicate electronically with anyone else in Tulsa.

21

Inside a house across the street, members of the white mob broke in and entered with torches. In that house, oblivious to them were a mother and four children. They saw the 4 men coming in and based on their mother's intuition and instruction, and hid underneath the bed. The men looked around the house and saw no one. From underneath the bed, the dwellers saw them as they lit the curtains with their torches and left.

"They are gone!"

Yelled that mother.

Coincidentally, they were able to get out of the house alive speedily.

As they departed the scene, there lingered a stench like that of roasted meat. At the same time, multiple bodies were lying all over BWS. Klansmen were seen from the overlooking hill huddled around a huge burning cross. In contrast, as screaming were evaporating from within Greenwood.

Residents became restricted from returning to Greenwood during the burning and looting.

As in the case of Dick Rowland, many blacks worked in White Tulsa.

As unrest spread to that part of the city, many middle-class white families who employed black people in their homes as house cleaners, live-in cooks, and other servants got detained by members of the white mob.

These rioters demanded the families turn over their employees to get escorted to detention centers around the city. Many white families complied. Some refused, not wanting to lose that luxury of service. Coincidentally, those who did not comply with their demands became subjected to the attacks and vandalism in turn. Meanwhile, measures were taken to prevent help brought to the victims.

Thus, causing the terror associated with those riots to extend across the railroad tracks and elsewhere throughout Tulsa.

22

Even so, several black men had served in the military, and they were not just going to lay down and die. Most of them, already taken up arms, retaliated against the white mob. According to one black retaliator:

"Every time I saw a white man shot, I felt happy, and I "swelled with pride and hope for the race."

However, he later got arrested after being shot at by the white mob.

It took hours before the Oklahoma National Guard arrived with 109 troops from Oklahoma City by special train. Such was ordered in the governor. Why did this take so long? Some claimed he could not legally act until he had contacted all the appropriate local authorities, including the mayor, the sheriff, and the police chief.

Even so, his troops paused to eat breakfast and lollygag. It was said; He also summoned reinforcements from several other Oklahoma cities.

While all this was on pause, thousands of black residents had fled the city; another 4,000 persons were rounded up and detained at various centers. Unfortunately, under the martial law established that day, the detainees were required to carry identification cards. As many as 6,000 black Greenwood residents were interned at three local facilities. Even though the troops arrived at 9:29 a.m. martial law was not declared until 11:49 a.m. In addition, by noon, the troops had managed to suppress most of the remaining violence. A 1921 letter from an officer of the Service Company, Third Infantry, Oklahoma National Guard, who arrived previously on May 31, 1921, reported numerous events related to the suppression of the riot:

1. They took about 30–40 blacks into custody.
2. Putting a machine gun on a truck and taking it on patrol.
3. Being fired on by Negro snipers from the Mount Zion Church and returning fire.
4. Being fired on by white men.
5. Turning the prisoners over to deputies to take them to police headquarters.
6. Being fired upon again by negroes and having two N.C.O.s slightly wounded.
7. Searching for negroes and firearms.
8. By detailing a N.C.O. to take 170 Negroes to the civil authorities; and
9. Delivering an additional 150 Negroes to the Convention Hall.
10. White rioters were disarmed and sent home.
11. Blacks got locked up in determent centers.
12. Tactics were put in place to suppress the evidence regarding the torching of Black Wall Street.

Martial law was withdrawn Friday afternoon, June 4, 1921, under Field Order No. 7.

23

In retrospect, the demolition of Black Wall Street did not occur because Blacks found the recipe for success and ensured it was tasty. It happened due to whites' baked-in perception that African-Americans were second-class, and coincidentally out of line and needed to be forced back in their place, back into the era of slavery – when they owned nothing. As Junior said: Jim Crow crowed too loud, resulting in segregation.

The Greenwood district offered proof that black entrepreneurs were capable of creating vast wealth if they put their heart mind and soul into it. Their efforts surpassed the stereotypical phenomenon that blacks were inferior and could not amass great fortunes. In addition, if you see something that's exceptional, someone of a superior race – not Blacks, owns it. Primarily, because of - out of box thinking. Greenwood not only attracted over 600 businesses but also grew from a population of 18,182 in 1910 to at least 90,000 to 100,000" residents by 1920.

Not only that. It was said of Whites that the sudden wealth of Black Wall Street rivaled the "forty-niners" in California. Yet, because of their opulence, they got torched and massacred by the whites.

It was clear that those whites were not upward mobile - a community that decided to pull themselves up by their own bootstraps. They wanted to inherit where they didn't toil.

The destruction of Black Wall Street was their target. Their rationale: It was a necessary and natural response to put them Blacks back where they belonged.

However, it must be noted, that whenever blacks gain a strong foothold in any endeavor, the rest is world-shattering mainly because they have the power within to effect meaningful change.

THE SOUL OF BLACK WALL STREET

THE AFTERMATH

23

Over 300 blacks died in the riot. While at least 10,000 families were left homeless. Moreover, at least 600 businesses got destroyed with an estimated $5 Million in damages.

The economy came to a grinding halt. There was a drought for essential workers, which caused white businesses to suffer. The once employed blacks had to wear unique tags signed by their white employers.

The Red Cross pitched in, providing food, tents, and meds. Booker T. Washington High School got transformed into a Hospital.

Most victims of the riot now lived in tent cities. B.C. Franklin, who had just moved to Greenwood three months ago, got displaced and pitched a tent – while seeking justice for black residents. During the riot, Franklin, an activist, and excellent attorney became a hero. He found himself calling until he was hoarse for restraint -- reminding the aggrieved "that two wrongs do not make a right." His law office got torched in the riot.

No insurance claims got paid. The blacks who returned did not return to homes they had on that Tuesday afternoon but most to ashes. They were also unable to find their possessions.

A. J, left Tulsa and never returned after an indictment got returned against him.

A grand jury was set up to investigate. They claimed blacks brought it on themselves.

Dick Rowland left town. He got saved from the torching of Greenwood.

A reconstruction committee got codified as pledges surfaced to rebuild. However, Whites stole the land in the reconstruction process.

Most of the bodies were never recovered, presumed to have been buried in a mass grave that has still never been located. In addition, no one was ever prosecuted or punished for the biggest racial massacre in American history.

In the final analysis, 35 city blocks lay in ruins, 1,256 residencies destroyed, and about 800 people hospitalized. Casualty counts varied; the dead got hastily buried in unmarked graves around the city.

Ironically, Funerals were forbidden. While only 36 deaths were confirmed at the time, historians hold firm that at least 300 civilians got murdered.

24

The Tulsa Tribune as customary railed against the black community. They made no apology to the police commissioners or to the mayor of Tulsa for having pled with them to clean up the cesspools in this city. They saw blacks as a race that deserved to have nothing just like they did when they got thrown into slavery. Moreover, nothing was going to change that no matter how much blacks elevated themselves.

A now-legendary editorial on June 4, 1921, editions of the Tulsa Tribune summed up the sentiments of most Tulsans.

"In this old Niggertown were a lot of bad niggers and a bad nigger is about the lowest thing that walks on two feet. Give a bad nigger his booze and his dope and a gun, and he thinks he can shoot up the world. Moreover, all of these four things can be found in 'Niggertown'—booze, dope, bad niggers, and guns.

With blacks now confined to tent living, the county commissioners at that time proposed to buy the land pennies on the dollar and sell the scorched lands to the highest bidders. On top of that, deal, Tulsa's power structure began to enforce various fire ordinances to prevent landowners from ever rebuilding. Those caught rebuilding would get arrested.

Also attached to this decree was the clause that any new structure would have to get constructed from fireproof materials. The Acme Brick Company, located near the Booker T. Washington High School in the Greenwood District, was instructed not to sell its products, as well as nearby lumberyards also refused to sell to blacks. Attorney B. C. Franklin, who represented most of these clients, advised them to build with anything, even orange crates. Meanwhile, the county offered jobs to the now- unemployed black Tulsans. However, many refused to clean up the debris left by the mob.

25

After the dust settled from that riot, a Grand Jury indicted John the Baptist as one of the instigators of the disturbance. While many begged to defer, he attempted to mediate with the officials in Tulsa to prevent the confrontation. Nevertheless, he sensed it D.O.A. They became set on blaming the black man – any and every black man.

Plus, Joh the Baptist stood up to them. It was beyond him to take systemic racism lying down. Consequently, he got viewed as a trouble-maker as a trouble maker. In addition, John the Baptist was a very successful and rich Black man who, through his financial independence, was able to fight back against such racism. He was not afraid to get into trouble - good trouble.

Leadership is what helps something grow or dissolve. Strong leadership or weak leadership are some of the main factors in shaping a community. John the Baptist, William T., A. J., and others all showed strong leadership in the Greenwood, playing a crucial part in its development. On the other hand, the white part of Tulsa lacked direction. A thing they coveted from the blacks in Black Wall Street.

As for those Black Wall Street's principal architects, they fled Greenwood, along with other residents like the Tulsa Star publisher A.J. Eventually, Tulsa's police tried to blame both A. J., and John the Baptist as agitators of the riot. Both had become known for challenging the uglier facets of white authority like segregation and lynchings and were indicted among dozens of Greenwood citizens.

William T. became a witness in the prosecutor's grand jury case, testifying on behalf of A. J., and John the Baptist had given orders to angry Blacks congregating and looking to defend Rowland from his lynching. A few whites Tulsans got indicted, but none of them were ever convicted.

After years of economic success in the thriving Black district, these entrepreneurs lost all they had built after an angry white mob attacked and set fire to the Greenwood district, burning everything to the ground. Combined, they lost millions of dollars in the 1921 race war

With nothing left of Black Wall Street but ashes, William T. left Greenwood for Los Angeles. John the Baptist headed to Independence, Kansas, and then to Chicago.

It was rumored that William T. had been lynched by a white mob in the race war, but it surfaced that he exiled himself to California.

Junior Rowland became Missing In Action.

THE EPILOGUE

26

A Black American from the grassroots rose to fame in 1947. He, no doubt, learned the concepts, which built Black Wall Street, only to be cut down by whites through the inhumane killing process known as lynching. I have chosen to call him L.B. His fabric got stitched among those thousands of lynchings in that new memorial staged in Montgomery, Alabama.

L.B., endowed with a cause greater than himself, defied the odds against black men and built for himself multiple successful businesses during that entire John Crow era. The brother worked hard, burning the midnight oil and generated more money than most whites in his community could shake a stick at - an enterprising adventure that could have caused his lynching in 1947.

Allegedly, L.B. got shot by his white neighbor and possibly other accomplices. Even so, his shooters never got persecuted. Unfortunately, no one did. The perpetrator later got released on a $2500 bond. That is all.

The *News* circulated and marinated in the press for weeks: *Enraged whites, jealous over the business success of a negro - slugged the 34-year-old, by a shot gunshot as well as pistol shots.* The incident occurred about 150 yards from L.B.'s establishment.

How did L.B. acquire his wealth? Was it based on the same principles of prestige and entrepreneurship implied by the blacks who inhabited Black Wall Street in the 1920s?

L.B. had a small trucking business and frequently hauled cattle to the Montgomery, Alabama stockyards. Multiple farmers hired him to feed and haul animals to the stockyard to sell. As his reputation for reliability spread like wildfire, many whites began to patronize him. Substantial success in business allowed L.B. to buy his first tractor-trailer truck.

After purchasing the tractor-trailer, the "short truck" became the "milk truck." *Everywhere it was milk.* He employed drivers to pick up milk from the sharecroppers and dairies and transport the liquid to the big dairy at Whittle. The endeavor provided a needed source of income, mainly when cotton was out of season, and the gins lay idle. His clientele worked hard toward earning them monthly what some called *milk checks* and L.B. was delighted to go to town on *check day*.

Eventually, L.B. earned the reputation of being a philanthropist and the talk of the town. People often commented:

The only way L. B. would not help you is that you didn't ask.

If a person did not have money, L.B. would let him/her ride free. And, if someone could not repay a loan, L.B. canceled the debt entirely. He employed farmhands and grew many plants, including cotton, corn, sugar cane, millet, and peanuts. Further, he raised livestock such as hogs, cows, goats, geese, guinea, and chickens.

Eventually, his trucking business was so successful that he bought a brand-new tractor-trailer and hired

more drivers. He was known to pay well and often better than the white farmers did. He even provided a place for his employees to live. He often said: *as long as a man will work, he has a place to stay.*
After acquiring property and establishing a multiple-use general merchandise store with a gasoline tank -
Jealousy within that neighborhood multiplied. The perpetrator who worked at the yard passed daily in front of his establishment and no doubt noticed his progress and so, he plotted.
It got rumored that L. B. insulted his wife, but those who knew better said that L.B. had class and business savvy and, as a result, was above such. According to one of the villagers: *That White man saw him as a way too successful negro.*
Now in conjunction with all those terror lynchings, from those over 800 counties, his name lies - staged.
Even though L.B. did not coexist in Tulsa, Oklahoma, but later in Montgomery, Alabama - his skillset of entrepreneurship and prestige cut from the fabric of Black Wall Street even if he did not belong.

About The Author

John A. Andrews, screenwriter, producer, playwright, director, and author of several books. As an author of over 60 books in the genre on relationships, personal development, faith-based, and vivid engaging novels. Also, a playwright and screenwriter.

THE SOUL OF BLACK WALL STREET

John is sought after to address success principles to young adults. He makes an impact in the lives of others. Mainly because of his commitment to making a difference in his life and the world.

Being a father of three sons propels John even more in his desire to see teens succeed. Andrews, a divorced dad of three sons Jonathan 24, Jefferri 22, and Jamison 19, was born in the Islands of St. Vincent and the Grenadines. His two eldest sons are also writers and wrote their first two novels while teenagers. He is elated, collaborating with Jonathan on a fourth title.

Andrews grew up in a home of five sisters and three brothers. He recounts: "My parents were all about values: work hard, love God, and never give up on your dreams."

Self-educated, John developed an interest in music. Although lacking formal education, he later put his knowledge and passion to good use, moonlighting as a disc jockey in New York. It paved the way for further exploration in the world of entertainment. In 1994 John caught the acting bug. Leaving the Big Apple for Hollywood over a decade ago not only put several national T.V. commercials under his belt but helped him to find his niche. He also appeared in the movie John Q starring Denzel Washington.

His passion for writing started in 2002 when he got denied the rights to a 1970's classic film, which he so badly wanted to remake. In 2007, while etching two of his original screenplays, he published his first book, "The 5 Steps to Changing Your Life" The rest is Historic.

Currently, with several of his titles in the movie and T.V. pipeline, John is directing his first film.

See IMDB: http://www.imdb.com/title/tt0854677/.

Visit: www.JohnAAndrews.com

THE UNITED STATES PANDEMIC

FIGHTING THE INVISIBLE ENEMY

FROM THE AUTHOR OF *PANDEMIC WARFARE*

JOHN A. ANDREWS

"A MEDICAL THRILLER"

THE AFTERMATH OF COVID - 19

THE SOUL OF BLACK WALL STREET

THE SOUL OF BLACK WALL STREET

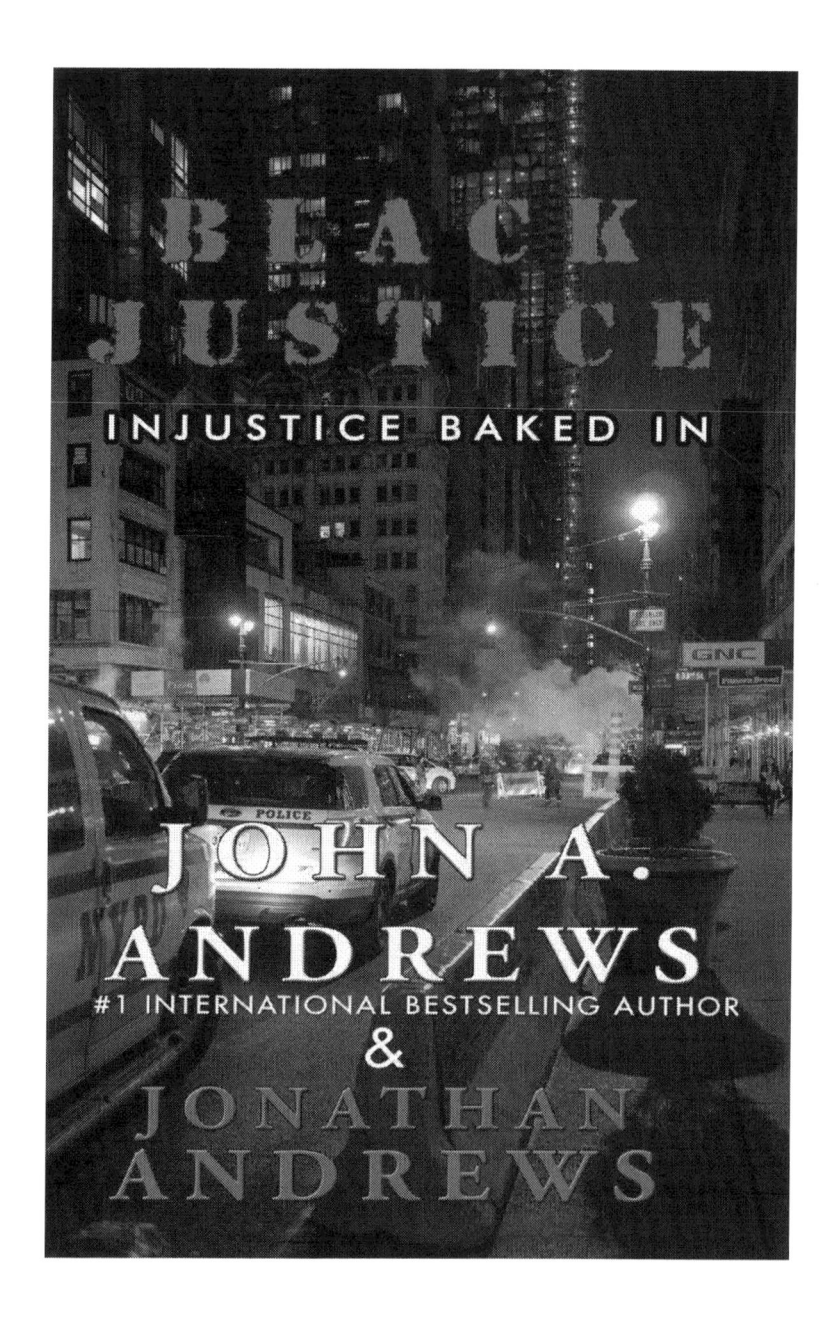

THE SOUL OF BLACK WALL STREET

THE BOTCHED AMENDMENT

JOHN A. ANDREWS

#1 INTERNATIONAL BESTSELLING AUTHOR

SUPPRESSING THE BLACK VOTE

THE SOUL OF BLACK WALL STREET

CHASING DESTINY

JOHN A. ANDREWS

#1 INTERNATIONAL BESTSELLING AUTHOR

GOT TO HAVE IT

THE SOUL OF BLACK WALL STREET

YEARNING TO EXHALE

FIGHTING THE INVISIBLE ENEMY

A NOVEL

JOHN A. ANDREWS

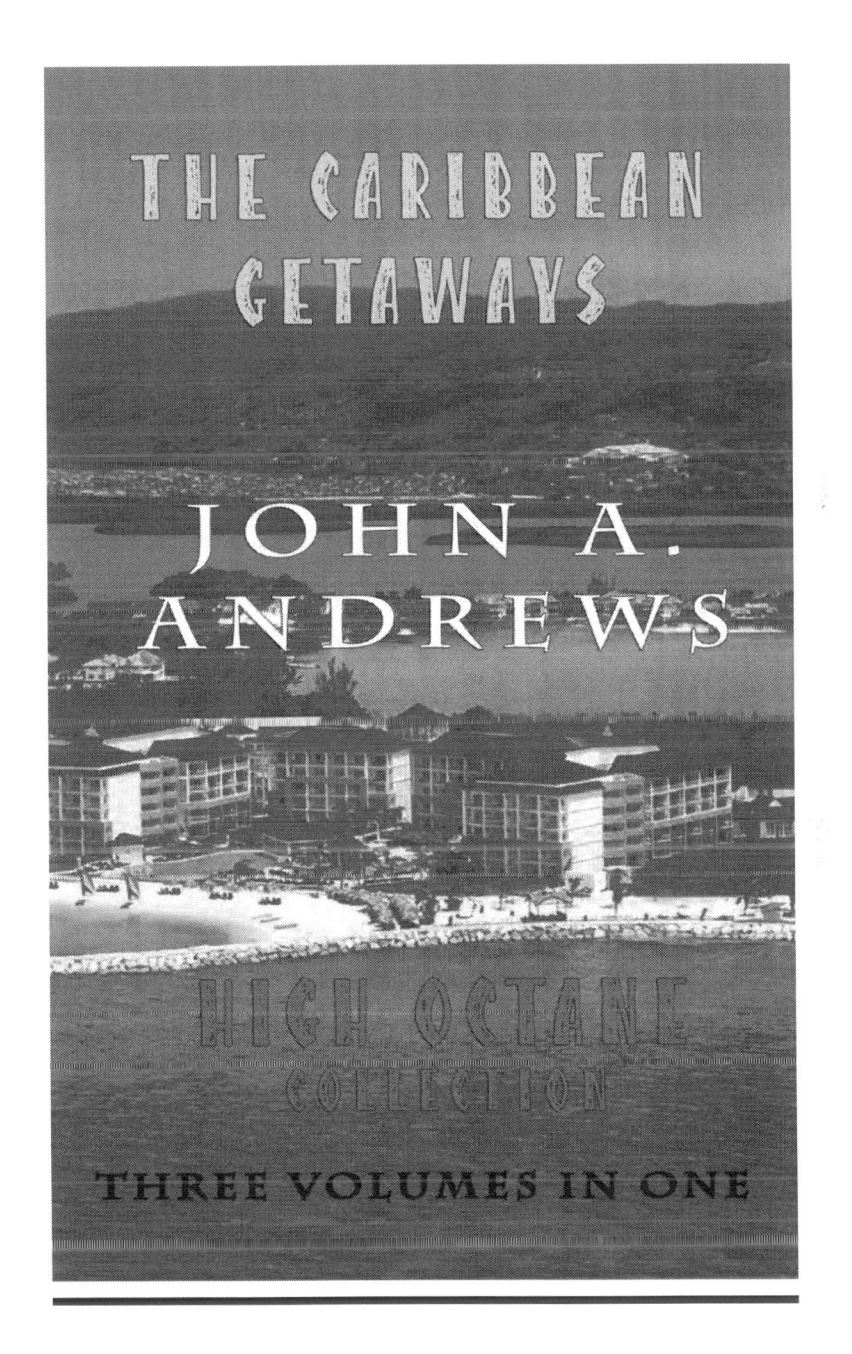

…

THE SOUL OF BLACK WALL STREET

THE MACOS ADVENTURE II

THE AUTHORITY SQUAD

SPECIAL EDITION

JONATHAN ANDREWS
JEFFERRI ANDREWS
With
#1 International Bestselling Author
JOHN A. ANDREWS

THE SOUL OF BLACK WALL STREET

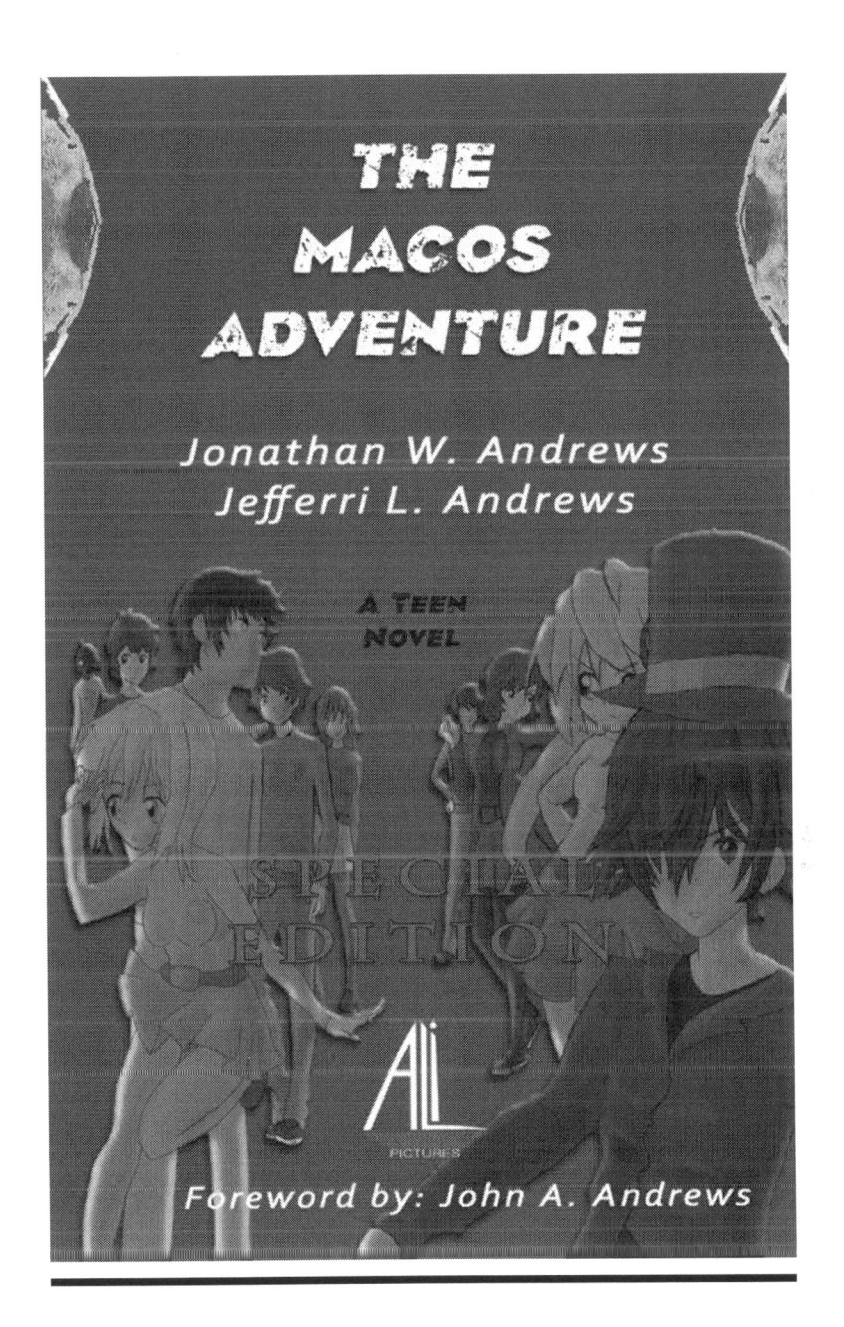

THE MACOS ADVENTURE

Jonathan W. Andrews
Jefferri L. Andrews

A TEEN NOVEL

SPECIAL EDITION

ALL
PICTURES

Foreword by: John A. Andrews

JOHN A. ANDREWS

NEW YORK CITY BLUES

THE UNDERGROUND OPERATION
A NOVEL

ONE FOOT IN *NEW YORK UNDERCOVER*
THE OTHER IN *ALFRED HITCHCOCK PRESENTS*

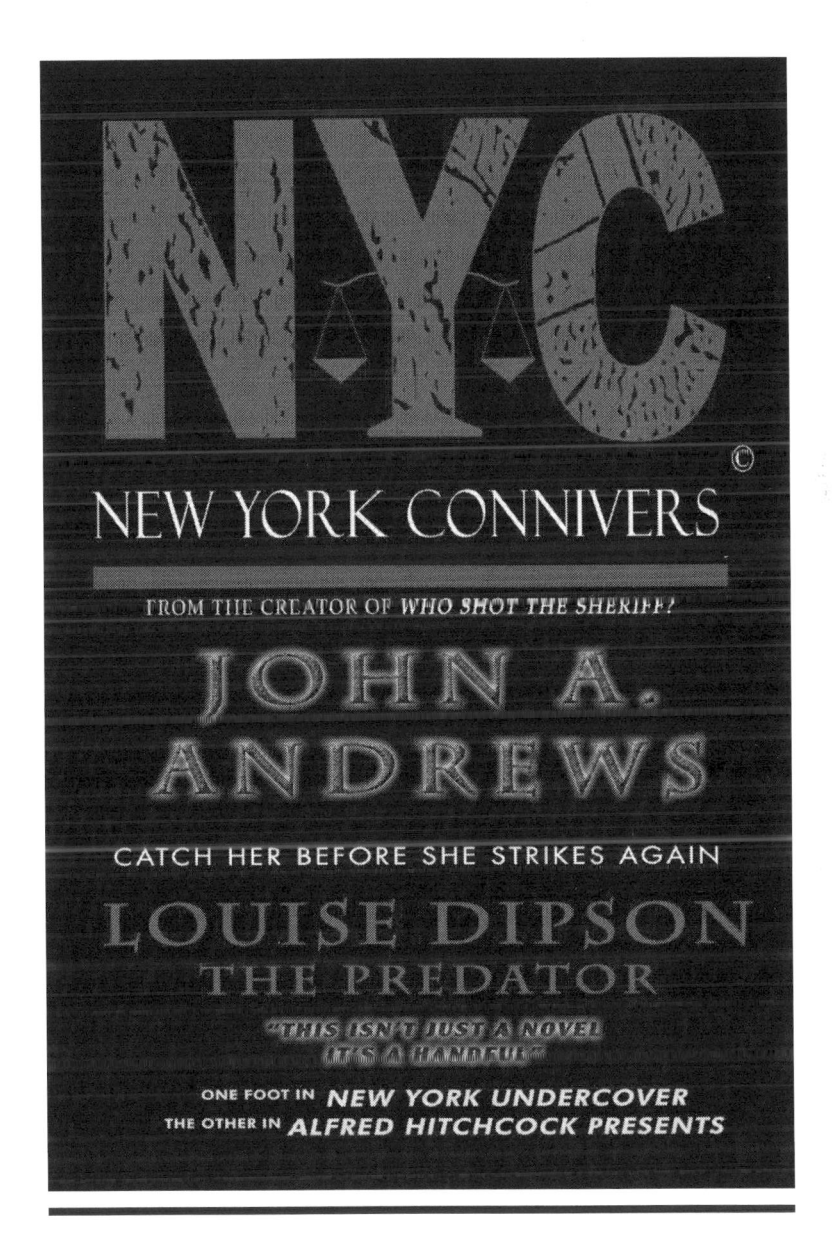

THE SOUL OF BLACK WALL STREET

NYC

NEW YORK CONNIVERS

FROM THE CREATOR OF *WHO SHOT THE SHERIFF?*

JOHN A. ANDREWS

CATCH HER BEFORE SHE STRIKES AGAIN

LOUISE DIPSON
THE PREDATOR

*"THIS ISN'T JUST A NOVEL
IT'S A HANDFUL"*

ONE FOOT IN **NEW YORK UNDERCOVER**
THE OTHER IN **ALFRED HITCHCOCK PRESENTS**

NYC

NEW YORK CONNIVERS ©

FROM THE CREATOR OF *WHO SHOT THE SHERIFF?*

JOHN A. ANDREWS

UNTIL DEATH DO US PART

A NOVEL

ONE FOOT IN **NEW YORK UNDERCOVER**
THE OTHER IN **ALFRED HITCHCOCK PRESENTS**

THE SOUL OF BLACK WALL STREET

THE SOUL OF BLACK WALL STREET

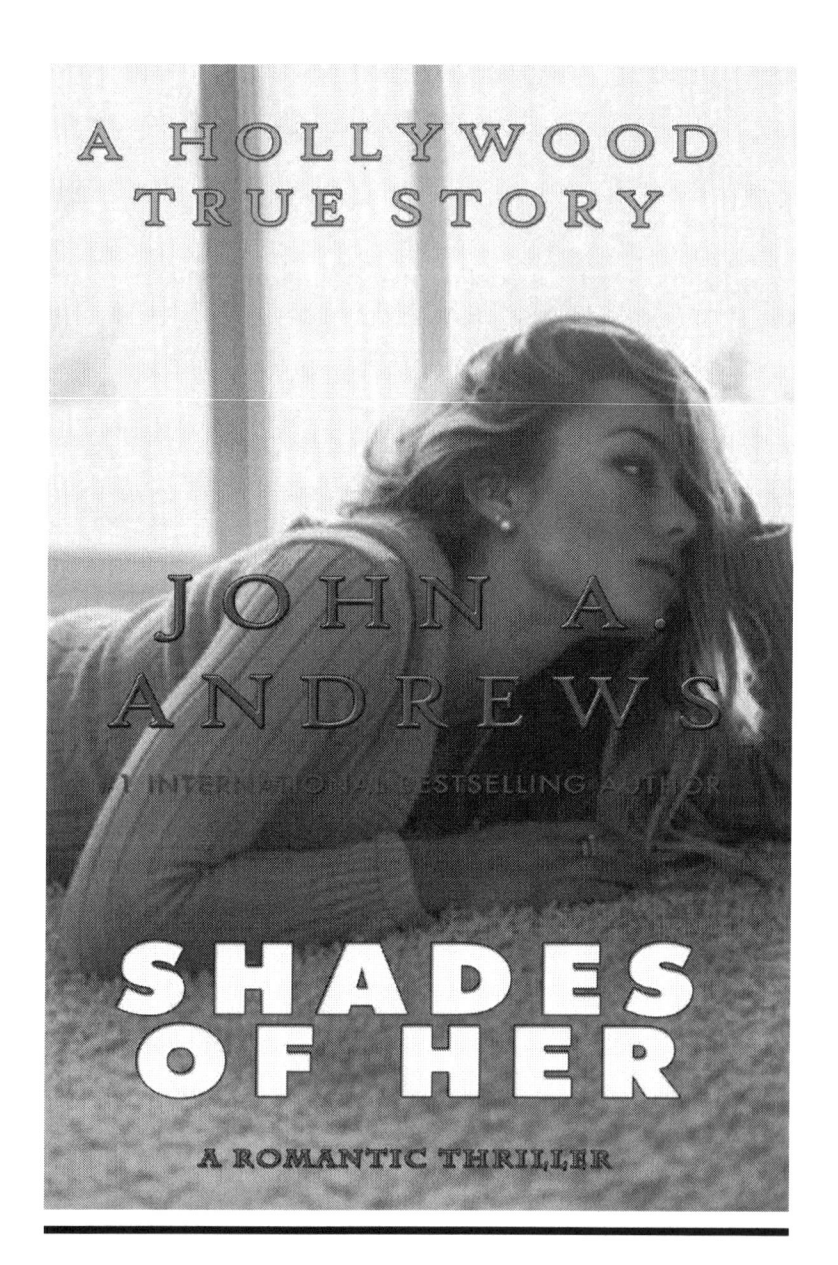

A HOLLYWOOD TRUE STORY

JOHN A. ANDREWS

INTERNATIONAL BESTSELLING AUTHOR

SHADES OF HER

A ROMANTIC THRILLER

Spread Some
LOVE
RELATIONSHIPS 101
AVAILABLE ON DVD
JOHN A.
ANDREWS

I'M STILL STANDING
WHEN THE DUST SETTLES
starring
John A. Andrews
BIOGRAPHY REVISED

The FIVE "Ps" FOR TEENS

National Bestselling Author
John A. Andrews

THE 5 STEPS TO CHANGING YOUR LIFE
BY: JOHN A. ANDREWS

"SEE YOU AT THE SUMMIT"

THE SOUL OF BLACK WALL STREET

ECLECTIC QUOTES

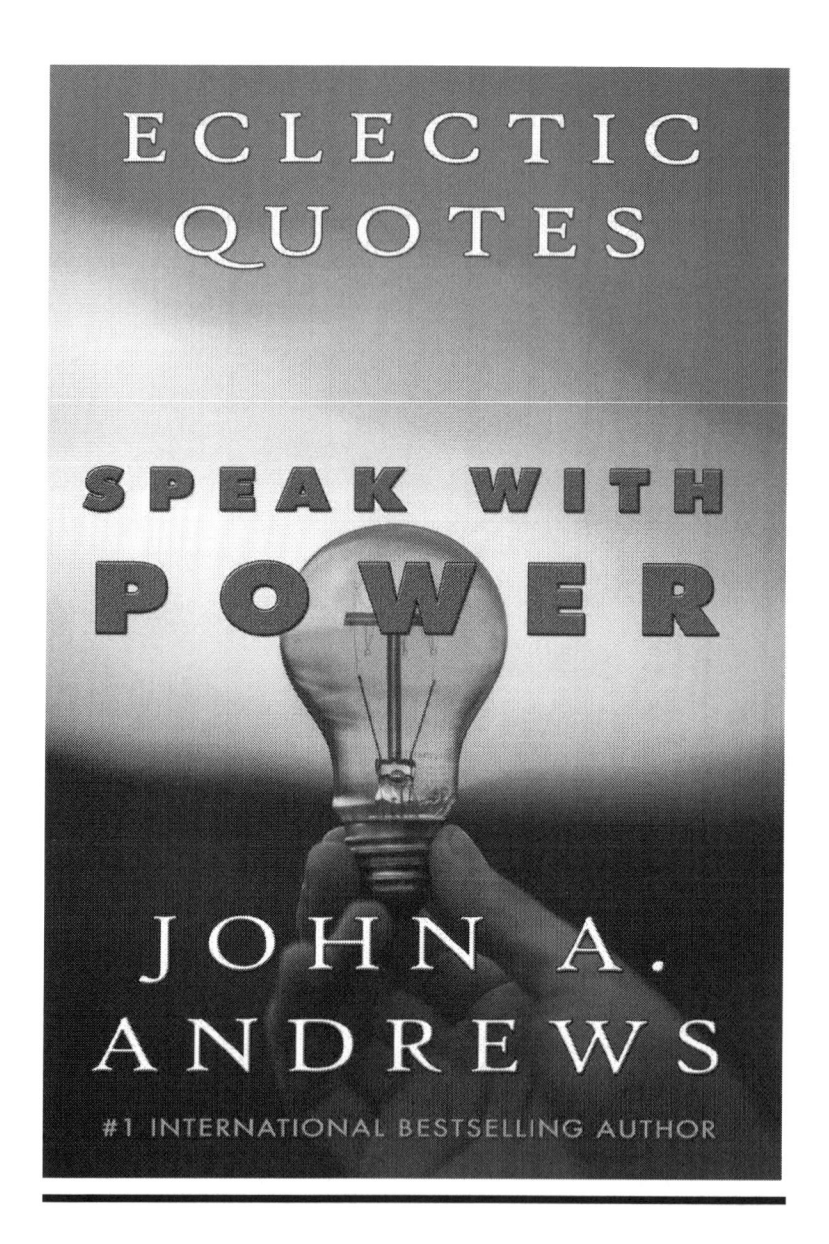

SPEAK WITH POWER

JOHN A. ANDREWS

#1 INTERNATIONAL BESTSELLING AUTHOR

THE SOUL OF BLACK WALL STREET

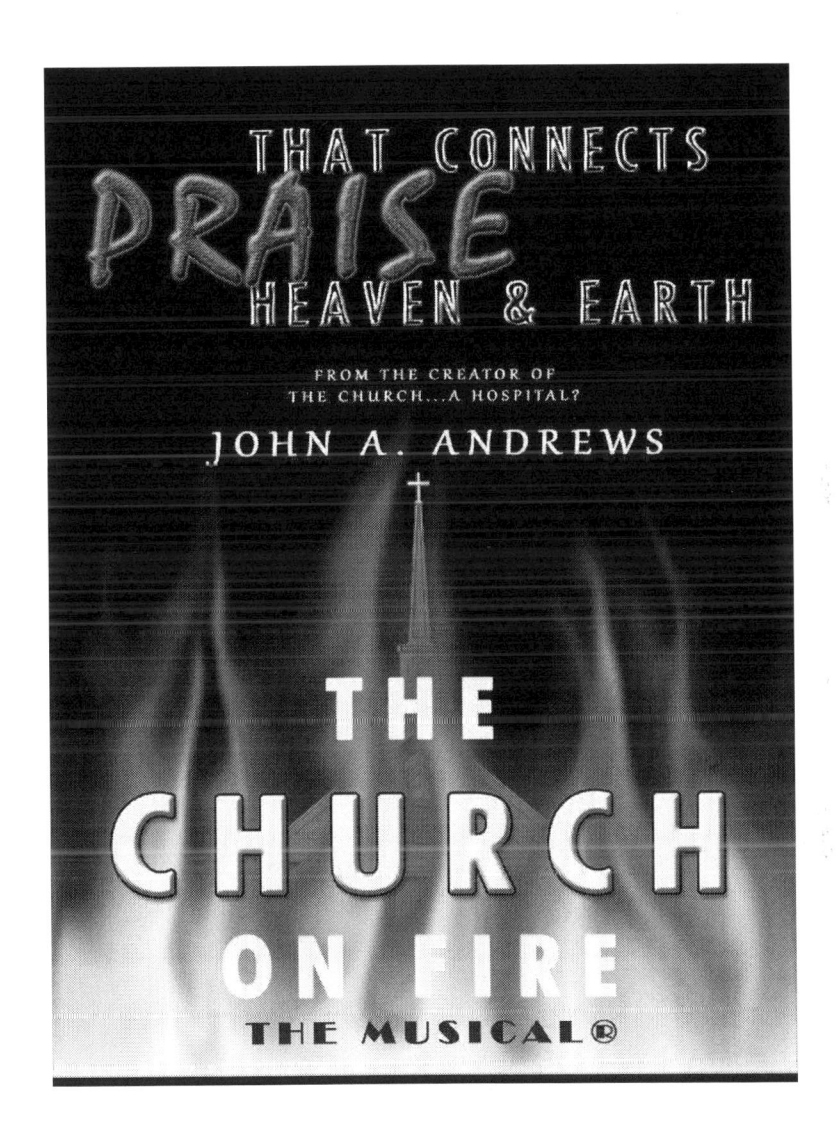

THE SOUL OF BLACK WALL STREET

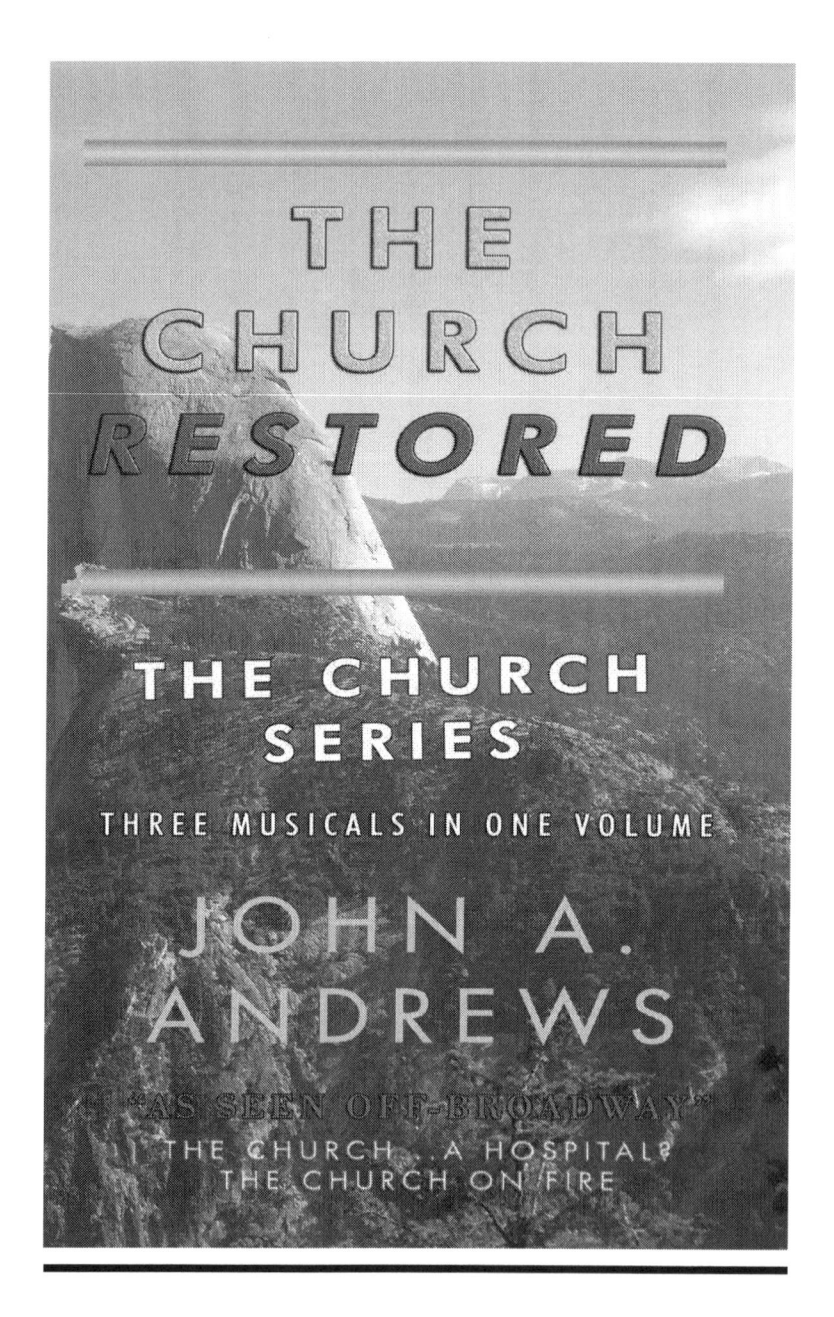

THE CHURCH RESTORED

THE CHURCH SERIES

THREE MUSICALS IN ONE VOLUME

JOHN A. ANDREWS

"AS SEEN OFF-BROADWAY"
THE CHURCH...A HOSPITAL?
THE CHURCH ON FIRE

Climbing Up From The Bottom **AUTHOR**

JOHN A. ANDREWS

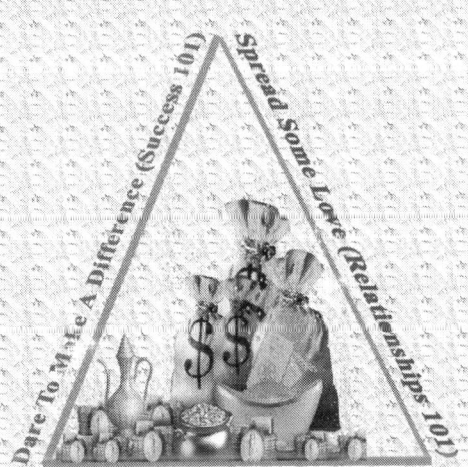

Spread Some Love (Relationships 101)
Dare To Make A Difference (Success 101)

The 5 Steps To Changing Your Life

THE SUCCESS TRIANGLE™

Three Books In One Volume
Including **DARE TO MAKE A DIFFERENCE**

THE SOUL OF BLACK WALL STREET

PRAISE THAT CONNECTS HEAVEN & EARTH

JOHN A. ANDREWS

CREATOR OF:
THE CHURCH ... A HOSPITAAL?
&
THE CHURCH ON FIRE

TOTAL PRAISE

MY UTMOST...

THE MUSICAL

BASK IN A SUPERNATURAL PRAISEWORTHY LIFESTYLE

THE SOUL OF BLACK WALL STREET

THE SOUL OF BLACK WALL STREET

A SNITCH ON TIME

DA POLICE

It's Nothing New For a Black Man Without a Gun To be Killed...

Writer & Director
JOHN A. ANDREWS

JOHN A. ANDREWS

The Church Is A Hospital?

THE MUSICAL®

**FROM THE CREATOR OF
RUDE BUAY
THE WHODUNIT CHRONICLES
&
THE CHURCH ON FIRE**

SO MANY ARE TRYING TO GO TO HEAVEN
WITHOUT FIRST BUILDING A HEAVEN
HERE ON EARTH...

#1 INTERNATIONAL BESTSELLER

How I Wrote 8 Books In One Year
JOHN A. ANDREWS
8
A
Author of
TOTAL COMMITTMENT
The Mindset Of Champions

THE SOUL OF BLACK WALL STREET

AGENT
O'GARRO
TIME IS THE ENEMY
A THRILLER
COMING
SOON
FROM THE CREATOR OF
RUDE BUAY
RENEGADE COPS
DESIREE O'GARRO
&
WHO SHOT THE SHERIFF?
JOHN A
ANDREWS
#1 INTERNATIONAL BESTSELLER

#1 INTERNATIONAL BESTSELLING AUTHOR
SHATTERPROOF
RUDE BUAY®
3
JOHN A. ANDREWS

THE SOUL OF BLACK WALL STREET

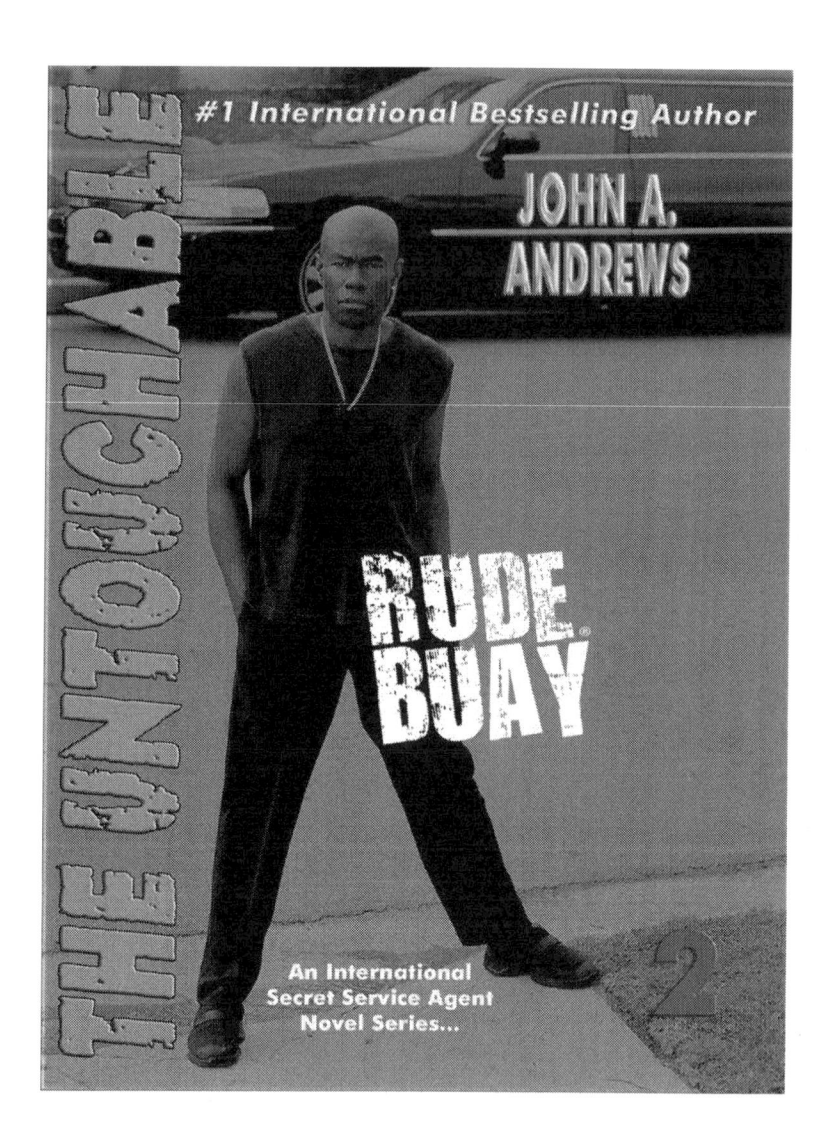

THE SOUL OF BLACK WALL STREET

NACIONAL SUPERVENTAS
CHICO RUDO
EL IMPARABLE
JOHN A. ANDREWS
THE UNSTOPPABLE

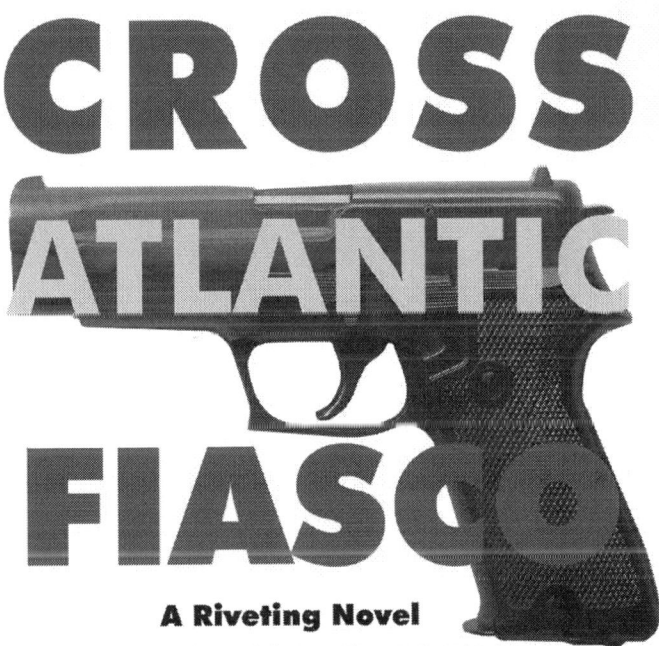

CROSS ATLANTIC FIASCO

A Riveting Novel

THREE EX-COPS, THEIR EX-BOSS, HIS 9 YEAR OLD DAUGHTER, AND THE BIGGEST BANK HEIST EVER ORCHESTRATED...

RENEGADE COPS

#1 INTERNATIONAL BESTSELLER

JOHN A. ANDREWS

Creator of
The RUDE BUAY Series
&
The WHODUNIT CHRONICLES

THE SOUL OF BLACK WALL STREET

THE SOUL OF BLACK WALL STREET

WHO SHOT THE SHERIFF?

II

Let THE GAMES Begin...

The MILTON ROGERS' CONSPIRACY

#1 International Bestselling Author

JOHN A. ANDREWS

Co-written with Teen Authors

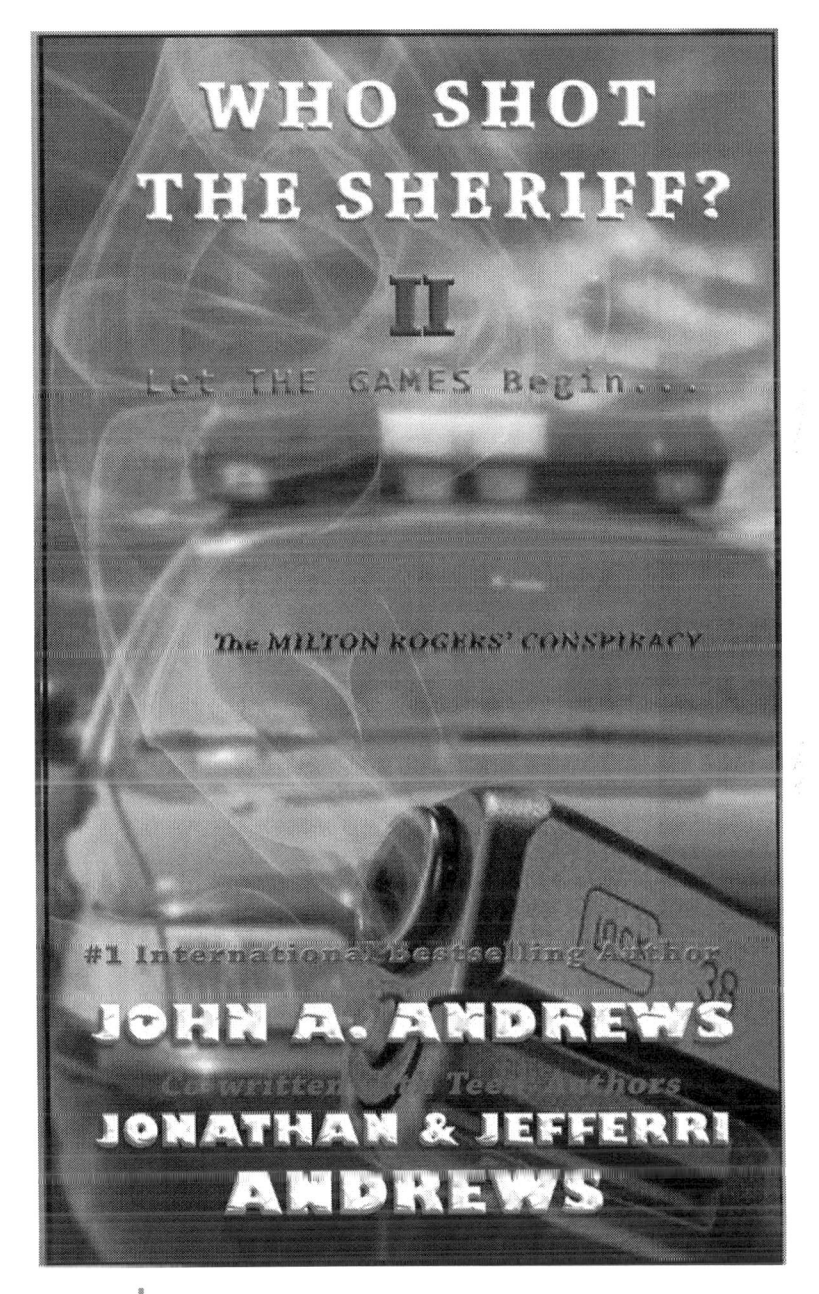

JONATHAN & JEFFERRI ANDREWS

WHO SHOT
THE SHERIFF?
The Hustle, The Flow, The Verdict.
#1 INTERNATIONAL BESTSELLER
JOHN A. ANDREWS
COMING SOON
To the Big Screen.
A 2016 A L I Pictures Production
PICTURES

DARE TO MAKE A DIFFERENCE

SUCCESS 101

FOR

ADULTS

#1 INTERNATIONAL BESTSELLING AUTHOR

JOHN A. ANDREWS

THE SOUL OF BLACK WALL STREET

By National Bestselling Author of Rude Buay ... The Unstoppable

TOTAL COMMITMENT
The Mindset of Champions

JOHN A. ANDREWS

COMING SOON

FIFTEEN IN TEN

JOHN A. ANDREWS
#1 INTERNATIONAL BESTSELLING AUTHOR

THE SOUL OF BLACK WALL STREET

JUNIOR

FROM THE ASHES OF GREENWOOD

A NOVEL BY
JOHN A. ANDREWS
#1 INTERNATIONAL BESTSELLING AUTHOR

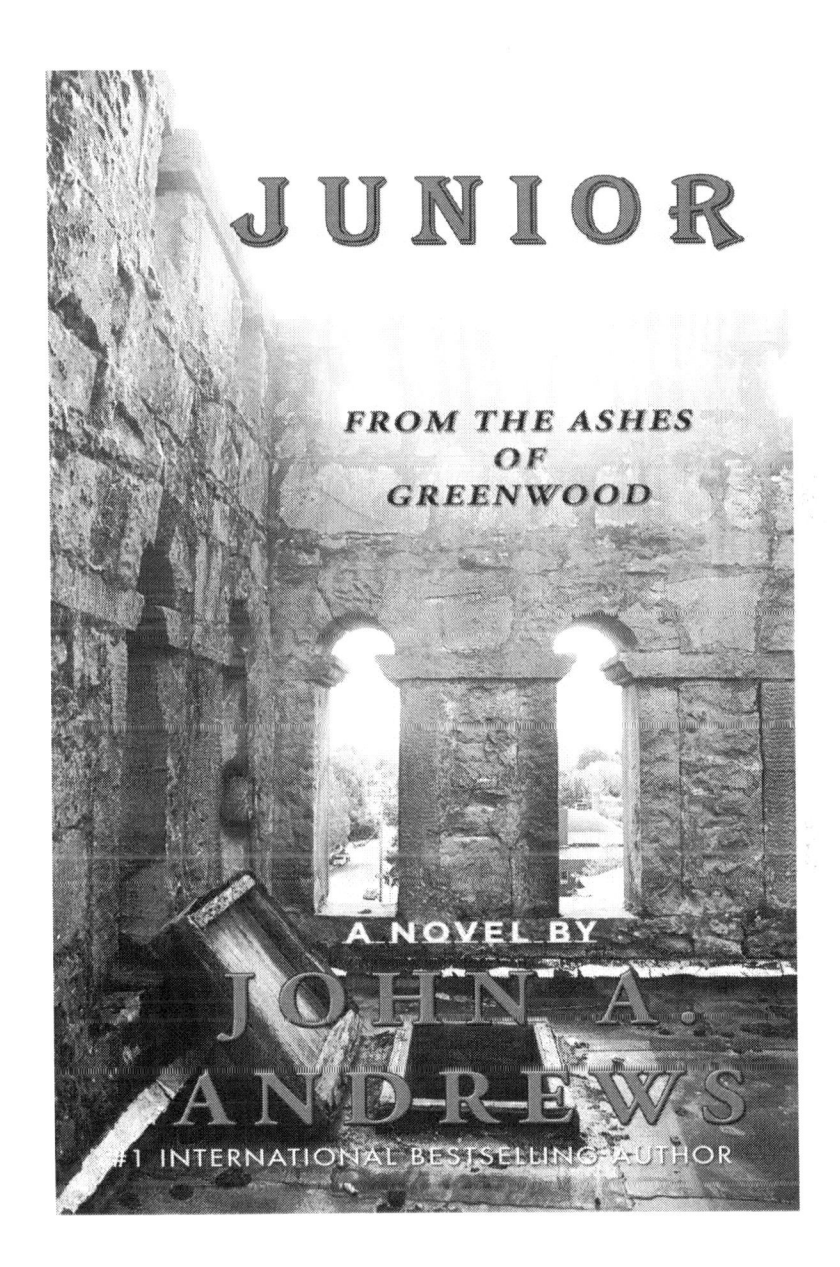

RUDE BUAY IV

CHASING THE DRAGONS

JOHN A. ANDREWS

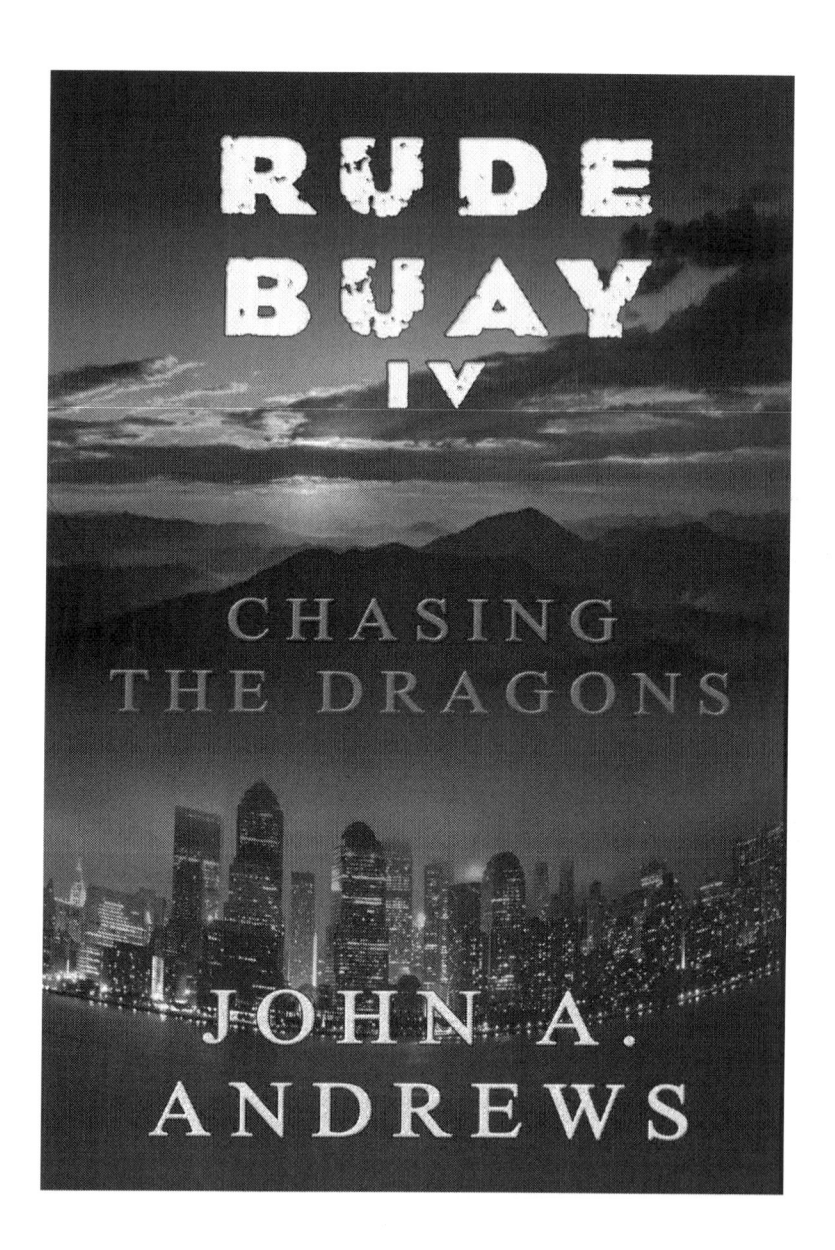

LADERA HEIGHTS

LA

UNDERCOVER

JOHN A. ANDREWS

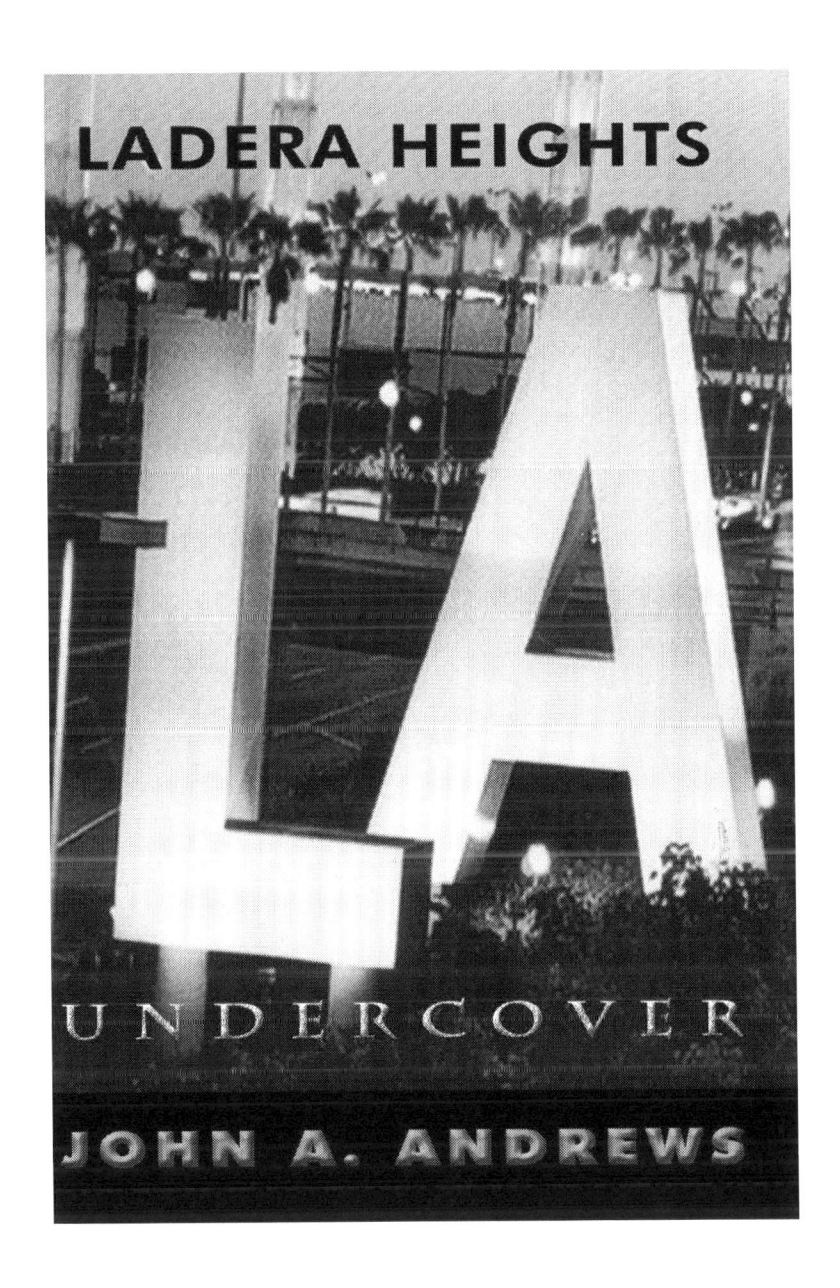

JOHN A. ANDREWS

#1 INTERNATIONAL BESTSELLING AUTHOR

The Untitled

HONG KONG

Novel

DESIREE O'GARRO
THE LETHAL KID

A TEEN THRILLER

FROM THE CREATORS OF
RUDE BUAY
AGENT O'GARRO
RENEGADE COPS
A SNITCH ON TIME
WHO SHOT THE SHERIFF?
&
THE MACOS ADVENTURE

#1 INTERNATIONAL BESTSELLING AUTHOR

JOHN A. ANDREWS
&
JEFFERRI ANDREWS

THE SOUL OF BLACK WALL STREET

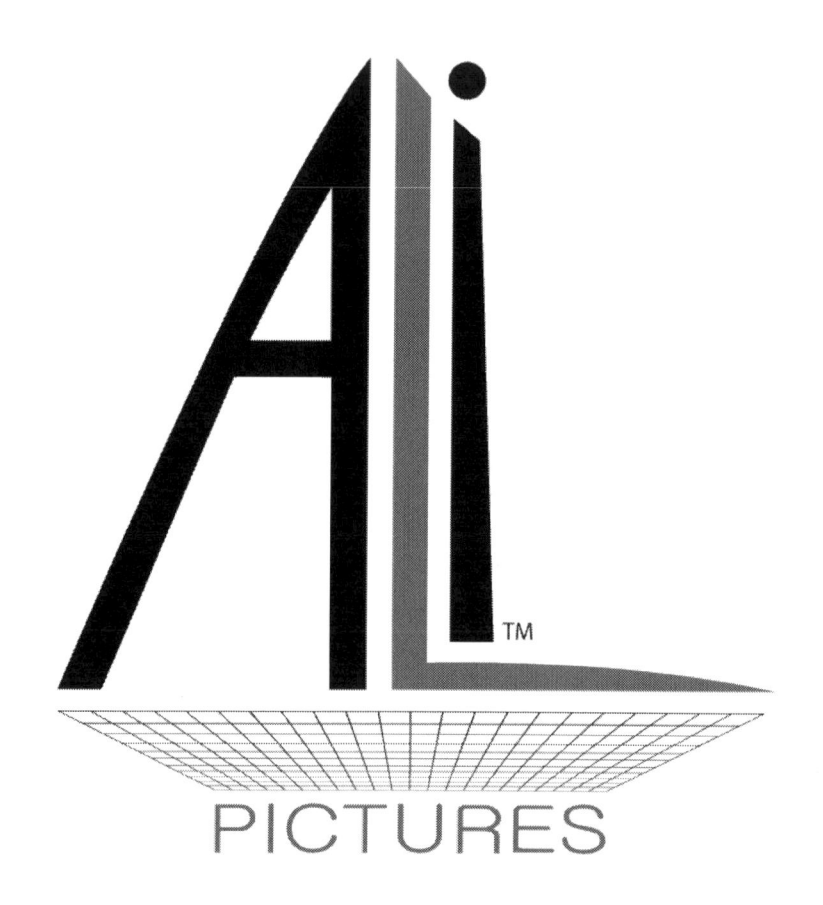

ALI PICTURES™

THE SOUL OF BLACK WALL STREET

UP ™

UNCANNY PICTURES

THE SOUL OF BLACK WALL STREET

THE SOUL OF BLACK WALL STREET

Made in the USA
Middletown, DE
19 May 2022